GENTLE

CATE DUNN

Copyright © 2017 Cate Dunn
All rights reserved.
ISBN:
978-0-6482102-0-7

This is a work of fiction. Names and characters are the product of the author's imagination and any resemblance to actual persons, living or dead, is entirely coincidental.

Cover Design: Bespoke Book Covers

A catalogue record for this book is available from the National Library of Australia

DEDICATION

For My Family

ACKNOWLEDGEMENTS

Leigh Mason, Julia Collins, Toni Fatherley, Anne Ellis, Thom Klein, Marilla North, Dymphna Cusack, Colleen Parker, Port Macquarie FAW, Turtles Book Club.

And this, our life, exempt from public haunt, finds tongues in trees, books in the running brooks, sermons in stones, and good in everything.   -William Shakespeare As You Like It

WAKING UP

In the light between wakefulness and sleeping, the young bride saw the woman in white who stood by her wedding bed. She watched as the apparition then lay at her side, dissolving into weeping. Amy held the secret visit close in the long years that followed, never forgetting the melancholy of the woman's movement nor the words she had no way to tell.

From on high, the river was a gold thread winding through the valley. The January floods had gone and the alluvial flats were green blankets of growth. From the plane's wingtip, Amy could see the main cottage surrounded by smaller cabins. Wide verandas fanned out from each building like open parasols parading their promise. This was The Retreat, where Amy imagined that the wash of loss she'd been carrying, might lift and melt away into the river and the forest beyond. But it was not a weekend solution of massage oil and wild rice which could heal a broken heart. What it could be, perhaps, was a step into something beyond herself into sanity. At least she hoped so.

Amy's own private war played out in the single room of memory of her ex-husband's philandering and her negligible status at investment firm, Goldworth and Finch. It led her to accept the special offer that popped up on the net. After all there was not a lot of promise to be had this Easter, only more broken promises to herself that she'd be alright. Here in the timber cottages spread out from the main house and meeting area, she hoped that even for a brief respite, a place was set aside for her to unwind the threads that had built to knot and strangle her insides.

The world she'd come from in Sydney, with its white knuckle competition and throwaway relationships, was a world away from the forest retreat that might reveal Amy to herself. She could trace her affliction back to childhood: not really understanding the motivation of others, not quick enough to duck and weave to get herself out of trouble. She looked back now and thought that maybe she was born without a protective shield. That somewhere in the DNA, some chromosome had cut loose and she was born into a world where lack of protection was dangerous, perhaps even deadly. Her attempts to communicate with her husband Mark were shut down before they had begun. The finalising of the divorce papers, was the final punctuation mark on his path to freedom and on her descent into self-abuse.

Mark had left with a, 'It's not you … it's me' excuse. It was so clichéd it hurt even more than the truth. It took a while to see the patterns which had been building for months before he left: the new suits, the early leaving and late returns with the excuse of work demands. 'You know how it is, Darling. There are no clocks at work. We stay until it's finished.' And that could be two in the morning if necessary, when a new case was underway. Amy understood the reality of the corporate world but what she couldn't fathom, was how the word 'Darling,' had become a weapon of deceit. A warming soother while the cat played the fiddle and her marriage broke apart. The sound of his new BMW echoed away down the drive and she found herself buried in work accounts, until the sight of the office sent her into palpitations and the strange looks of her co-workers signalled burn-out.

The main house looked like a timber Tardis, with its lighthouse cupola and its secret world inside. French doorways opened like cuckoo clocks into private spaces, with seatings for one. She wasn't sure that a wind down was possible for a mind imploding like hers. She remembered the final note from Mark which ended with 'Ciao.' So casual in its infidelity. And then the seismic market shifts that led her trading decisions in the firm to be off centre and into high risk territory. Amy was free-falling without a parachute, no longer able to deny the tidal wave on the horizon that had accelerated with Mark leaving her.

The facilitator was serene, which accentuated Amy's own wrinkled forehead and darting eyes. Beth had that look of exposure to vitality: the skin glowed along with her smile. In comparison, Amy's inner resolve was shattered. She guessed the receptionist had seen it before: the wringing hands on the desk as she answered the Welcome Questionnaire, the hollow smile that gestured defeat. 'You'll be in Cabin 3. The fire's on and there's purified water in the jug. We don't want you eating anything until dinner, so drink plenty of water, relax and we'll meet you back here in the common room at six.'

That was three hours without her usual sugar hit or afternoon alcohol fix and the panic felt ridiculous that it was so immediate and so intense. She guessed the food restriction was to expose just what it was she had stuffed down with her usual grazing of the fridge and the use of the key to the liquor cabinet. Layers of anxiety had become synonymous for normality as she pushed down her fears into a casual look around the centre. Cut timber was neatly stacked in a copper cauldron beside the fireplace, ready for the evening lighting. She felt drawn into collapsing into one of the leather armchairs that sat around the hearth. 'To sleep perchance to dream.' But not even the death of sleep would be enough to soothe the mind which ran amok, bouncing off self-doubt and ricocheting down corridors of why she'd let herself come here in the first place.

She managed to keep the filter on her mouth to not actually articulate Shakespeare but her stomach wouldn't comply and the gurgling continued as she made her way self-consciously towards her cabin. The room was cosy, if somewhat hermitage like. A single bed sat against the wall in the one room which held a friendly fire that welcomed her in. A timber bath beside the fire held the possibility of a soothing collapse into its warm waters. You came as an individual, which suited her. Couples were required to hire separate cabins. She considered that might heighten the tension for some. Still, it made sense to 'meet yourself' in a place structured for solitude, even if at the same time, there was no promise that whoever you might meet would be friendly or even safe.

Amy had always considered that danger lurked outside her control: the boss who ignored you after you turned forty, the last year's outfit which looked so yesterday today, the chemical infiltration that you have no control over when you don't know it's there when it's everywhere … in everything. Isn't it? The outside felt like it was invading even here. She checked as she felt her breath quicken and her head start to hurt. The junk inside seemed to understand that the zoo gates were abandoned and it was time to come out. No wonder Jerry at work had that look on his face that warned, 'Traders who burn out rarely return.' This wasn't a weekend retreat; it was a lifeboat and she was grabbing for the rope.

As she stared into it, the fire began to mirror the assault. She watched in the rising embers as the stories stirred into life and danced upon the coals in awakened fright. The agitation had been building, etching its way invasively into who to trust and how to act. She could sense the panic she couldn't suppress when it was time to sell at work. Jerry had said there was no room for negative emotion, just the high from a successful bid. But her emotions had failed her and now her baggage case was open and she felt she could lose control.

She unpacked recklessly, throwing jeans into drawers where cuffs curled out in unfinished business. A lamp stood by a wicker chair which she sat in for a few seconds before standing again to pace without purpose, except perhaps to lessen the agitation. When in doubt, do something even if it's meaningless. The alternative was to feel the clammy hands, the shortened breath, the round and round voices of accusation, 'You did this to yourself!' She succeeded in censoring, 'Loser' and 'Fool' as they surfaced but beyond that, the voices continued to fold into the cupboards of her memory along with her hopes.

From the seat by the window, Amy watched the other cabins' smoke lifting in the updrafts. She imagined each individual's breath inside, blowing away the reasons why they'd come here, rising in the smoke to settle in a haze above the valley. She imagined the river nearby, might capture that sediment as it fell and then wash it away. The river had burnt gold from the plane but now the sunset had it mirroring purples and crimson, the colours of the valley already starting to weave a tapestry of longing that was new to her.

It was autumn but she was resolved that she'd get in tomorrow and have a swim anyway. Wash away the blues. She knew there were platypus. Maybe this mixed-up creature might let her be part of its wild world … if she was quiet about it. But this was her Achilles, she knew. Being quiet had held her dumb when Mark had swum each morning at the Bondi pool with the co-worker stroking beside him. She could have queried the co-incidence as she sat sipping lattes. 'Is there something I should know, Mark? Would you even care if I swam beside you myself?' But it was all too late at the ending of her marriage and it was the silence of the apartment that greeted her when she'd return from work alone.

Mark's company, Harrison and Partners at Law, had a habit or unwritten policy, that the front woman was young and beautiful. She didn't need to be experienced. Mark would come home and share with Amy how amazed he was that Sarah was so quick to learn. How good she was with the clients. How she had even solved the computer problem which had infiltrated the files. Amy called her 'WonderWoman.com' as a joke but he didn't laugh and she felt stupid that her cut-off remark had seemed so petty.

She contemplated how a woman of Sarah's age could make a woman of Amy's age seem so infantile. But it was the same old music that had been played forever. The secretary knew it with the red Lycra swimsuit which clung to her wet nipples. Amy knew it too with the Scholl inserts and the promise to return to the gym tomorrow. Everyone knew it and particularly Mark, who saw his real chance to stay young. And why not after all those laps up and down to keep him looking like he deserved it? So, it was inevitable. But that birth defect she had where she wouldn't know a truck was bearing down until she stared into its high beam on impact, just kept it from her view.

Amy had been staring into the past for quite a while, when she realised that two eyes across the way in Cabin 2 were watching out as well. She wasn't sure who jumped into awareness first but there was embarrassment and then an acknowledgement that they had been both offloading thoughts and hadn't really seen each other until that moment of connection. She noted how his ginger hair matched his pale complexion, so unlike Mark's dark eyes and demeanour. He nodded and turned back from the window but she'd seen a flash of recognition in him that was more than the nod he gave on the airport bus getting here.

No-one came to The Retreat without reason, she thought. It wasn't a health farm for weight loss, not that that would hurt. Mark would catch her looking in the mirror sighing away and say she would look beautiful if she just lost a few kilos. She had to admit she wasn't as disciplined as he was but he would ignore her anyway when she dressed to please. So, where was the motivation? The black silk lingerie she bought too late was a second preference to the bottle of red he'd befriended and she'd find herself in bed with a good book instead.

Dinner was in the common room of the main house. They'd been asked to refrain from talking and to not make eye contact with anyone. 'For mindful eating,' Beth had said. That sealed the intent that Amy might be able to dodge any serious thoughts with casual remarks about the weather. She imagined the long hours ahead, without conversation, without TV or her phone which she had been required to leave at the desk at check-in. The weight of the emptiness to come was scary. She had tried to reassure herself, 'Just go to bed and sleep it off.' Habit had taught her that sleep was an uncertainty though and dread had turned the walls of her cabin into a prison like vice, squeezing her mind to mush.

With her eyes cast down and no alcohol allowed, what sprang to consciousness was what she had replied to Mark when he checked her about the third glass of wine at the Barrett's Christmas party, the night he had left her. 'I'm just keeping up with you.' She'd spoken as if it was a competition that they'd drink each other into the ground, or grave … whichever came first. It had only been the first five minutes into the evening at the retreat and the witchery of the weekend was already beginning to bubble. She wondered whether the people running the sessions were skilled enough to handle the machinations of the mind though, particularly when the vegan menu lacked any sophistication.

After dinner, Beth drew them to the fire. The three participants, smiling anxiously at each other, arranged themselves in the leather armchairs. There was an uncertainty to sit forward at attention or back to relax. Amy noticed that she had positioned herself at the edge of the chair in anticipation. One chair was empty and Amy had noted that four cabins made up the estate. She wondered if someone was late or if they had given up before they'd begun. It was understandable that to lift yourself out of the city and into the country with its wilderness extremes could heighten anxiety, not cure it. The man she'd seen from her cabin smiled at her but she turned, embarrassed at being recognised. What did he see in her? Was this any different to her past relationships? Who she was had become what someone else needed her to be, she realised. The sign above the fire read, 'Simply Me'. But now she questioned how simple could that really be?

Beth had urged them not to censor their thoughts and to simply let their minds run free. At The Retreat, participants were encouraged to discover parts of themselves through letting nature be their guide. She looked like she was an expert herself in self-management with her healthy glow. Amy wondered if it came naturally or if she had overcome bad habits herself. 'The space has been created to nurture and unfold, and the time over the long weekend at Easter, is given to allow you to be comfortable with what you find.' Beth spoke carefully to bring them into a place of calm, which had been missing for so long. Beth noticed that Amy's shallow breathing overshadowed any possibility of discovery so she tried to reassure her that she was safe. 'We hope you can accept and trust the process of discovery we have developed here. We are not here to give advice but to allow you to be a witness to your own feelings and to get to know your own identity. It's simple but it's also profound. We know it can help to change your life.'

Amy dwelt on any changes that would help but where and how these changes might occur she had no idea. Dreams that night consisted of a cave in which Mark and Sarah had locked her. She had loved Mark but couldn't equate his snide comments about, 'Letting herself go,' with their wedding vows to honour each other for better or worse. Amy felt she had kept to her promise but an insistent voice knocked on the cave door shouting, 'Wake up!' Not that she could hear it as a shout, as the rock face she thought, was obviously solid and interfering with the volume. But the repetitive urgency was sufficient for it to be the words in her consciousness that woke her in the morning, just as the bell was ringing for breakfast. What had changed, was that she had slept through the night for the first time since she could remember, and that alone held promise.

FOREST SOUND BATHING

The schedule read that today they were to listen. There was no expectation except for breakfast at seven. As Amy arrived in the common room, Beth introduced Sergio who was leading the group. 'For forest sound bathing.' Sergio was a musician whom Amy recognised from posters she'd seen around Bondi. He apparently lived in the valley. Beth and Sergio exchanged an intimate glance and Amy wondered what else they might have in common. She remembered watching Sergio set up at Sculptures by the Sea, the annual international sculpture event which had locals scrambling over the cliff faces to view sculptures that sat like sentinels over the Pacific Ocean. His last installation, 'The Watchers', had been acclaimed by tens of thousands of visitors for its interaction within the landscape. The instrument Sergio sculpted collected the wind and the wave sounds and amplified the natural world. She remembered thinking that maybe all you needed was a tall, dark musician to make sense of the world. She wondered what possibilities Sergio had already found in the valley and by degrees what possibilities she might find in herself.

Breakfast began with muesli, fruits and yogurt. The scrambled tofu and mushroom omelette was edible, as was the smoothie made from greens from the garden which surrounded the main house and cabins. Now that she had orientated herself, Amy saw that the retreat was shaped into the heart of the garden itself. The whole effect was circular with the gardens on the outer rim in radiating bands to the river and its windings beyond. A private space for reflection was built into the circular rhythms of plantings and growth. Amy considered that while she had sat at work for years behind her computer, calculating the next share price and the optimum time to sell, someone had been carving a design out of the rocks and timbers on the site. What a vision, to build a place where people were drawn to for healing! It felt like an antidote to what the city had become, a tangled network of excess.

After breakfast, Sergio led them into an abstract world of sound. On the veranda he played a mix of melodies on rock percussions, reed strings from the river and a wind instrument made from a hollowed log, similar to a didgeridoo. Amy thought that the ancient Aboriginal people who developed that instrument must have known something unique about the effect of sound on our mood. The haunting reverberations were playing her body as a sounding board and her body responded with an easing of her tension. She'd heard of Tibetan monks chanting, with the effect on heart rhythms remarkably similar.

'Your experience today is to enter the environment and discover what sounds you can. We will all share them after dinner.' Sergio seemed hopeful that they all could participate and learn something special about the natural environment and themselves as part of it. He was dark and tanned and looked like he'd spent a lot of time outdoors himself. Amy reflected on the way his hands became indivisible with the instrument, playing it as a living thing. What concerned her though was what living sounds might be pressing on the inside of her brain to get out. She'd heard the sound of her own internal scream and she knew that the queue of frustrations leading up to it would be exhausting.

The path, which led down to the river, had already carried someone before her. The grass had been flattened just recently and she saw that the fresh footsteps were those of someone who was barefoot. The others had headed towards the forest and along the other path to the hill. Trees, turning into autumn colours of russet and orange, lined the ridge. Amy wanted to be at the river first. The platypus, she hoped, might still be out and she knew that they disappeared into hollows in the banks if they were disturbed.

She tried to focus on the sound of the trickling which she could hear up ahead. The river was quite still at this point near the homestead where a swimming hole had formed. There was a jutting rock on the other side that she thought could be good for sunbaking on. She wasn't concerned about who else might be around as the retreat was far enough away from civilisation that only workers would be here. She guessed that maybe the footprints were those of one of the property hands.

She heard the splash and then the stroking of the swim. She stopped and imagined the sound of Mark again and sensed that this stroke had a stronger and more urgent rhythm than his. Mark would swim with such ease, the result of years of training at Bondi for ocean swims he usually won. His efficiency in the water matched the efficiency with how he conducted his life. It was the efficiency with which he had ended their fifteen year relationship. His was a smooth character in every way: promoted to partner before his fortieth birthday, his place in the law firm securing his status. But Amy gave Sarah a few years at most to see that his male gaze settled on a new object of desire for only so long, before shifting on to something more appealing. If anything was the Achilles heel for Mark, it was the infatuation of the chase which proved inconsequential on delivery. Mark's hunger for more was to be his undoing in the end.

As Amy reached the bank, the stranger was pulling himself onto the rock on the other side of the river. She sensed a restlessness in how he lifted himself out. She noticed the way his back muscles pulled tightly as he melded into the rock face, lizard like. He hadn't seen her and she hadn't seen him at dinner last night nor breakfast this morning. Closing her eyes to listen, as instructed, she could hear his panting at the exertion from the swim. It was interesting to listen without filters, she thought. There was an intimacy that didn't need an introduction.

She considered the project they'd been given: to find sounds that meant something to you. The last sounds from Mark to her were hateful really. She remembered sobbing in the open on the sands at Bondi while Mark berated her to get up. 'You look ridiculous, Amy. Get up and go home before you embarrass yourself anymore.' She remembered how he had tugged at her, pulling at her reluctant arm, showing some pretence of closeness to cover the mess of their relationship. But the local eyes they usually saw on their daily routines were detached in their response to his bullying.

Amy must have been staring abstractedly because she didn't notice the figure leave. She didn't know if he had seen her and if he did, what he made of the grimace her face must have contorted into in the memory of Mark's cruelty. She called out, 'Hello.' The sound of it echoed across the water and hit the cliff face on the other side, to then return again hollow. Something about the stranger had made her curious. She shook away the confusion that some kind of identity had arisen in the way the man had seemed so confident in his body. She wondered what it would be like to be able to just lift yourself up and out of the water with such ease and strength.

Her confidence had been locked away a long time ago when Mark had started to question what she was wearing and how she aged. She had resigned herself to not fitting into the Bondi scene. In truth, she didn't really care what the fashion was. She thought her money could be better spent elsewhere but Mark kept up with the latest. The Armani suit was the last purchase before the final goodbye. Amy still hadn't resolved how she didn't ask for anything they'd shared. He'd kept all the things they'd bought together. She just didn't have the strength to challenge any of it.

'Have you discovered anything interesting?'

It was the man from the window last night. His hair was greying, but Amy judged him about her age. There was an uncertainty in his manner, so different to Mark's sure presence and easy smile … when it pleased him to give it.

'Oh, I'm sorry. I didn't hear you come along the path. Did you come down that way from the house?' She thought that Liam, as he introduced himself, had been particularly quiet.

'No, I walked along the river bank. I found a gap in the forest and ended up following the river line till I got here. I heard you calling.'

'Someone was swimming. Did you see him?' She tried to sound nonplussed but the identity of the swimmer was urging her forward.

'Only Eileen who was looking like she was trying to make music from nature. It's all a bit New Age, don't you think?'

'Well, I've seen Sergio's work before and he's well regarded as a sculptor and a musician, so I'm willing to experiment.'

'What kind of music do you like, Amy? What kind of sounds do you expect to discover?' Amy wasn't sure what his interest in her was but she resolved to not be suspicious and just try and relax into the experience.

'I like The Blues. Maybe I'm a melancholy kind of gal.'

She tried to be light-hearted but held her head down and kicked the sticks on the bank into the water. She was too preoccupied with her own thoughts of the stranger anyway. Picking up some gumnuts lying at her feet in a random swoop she said she'd see him at the get-together that evening. 'Look forward to hearing what's out there to play music on,' she called back to him casually.

'And what's in here,' he replied, pressing his hands to his chest. There was a stillness in his gesture which she hadn't expected. Such an open expression of emotion. Another enigma from the distant glances he'd given before. She chastised herself for being so superficial when others were willing to take a chance. She recognised the old Amy who wouldn't know a conversation if her mouth was let out on day leave.

Alone, the rest of the day felt dreamlike. She'd entered the bush and had discovered pockets of rainforest. Some of the trees had buttress roots that stood into the earth like a claw. She thought of how the tree inside had been strangled so the strangler fig could grow. Some seed of fate had lodged at its base and then over time it had grown to overtake its host. She thought about the chaotic nature of life and how we didn't have much chance against the forces that were silently operating on us. The sounds of the forest were the monkey vines squeaking as they rubbed against each other in the slight wind that had come up. The tops of the canopy brushed together but otherwise down here amongst the ferns and rotting leaves, the world was quiet. She felt some seed inside herself was beginning to sprout and she remembered the gumnuts in her pocket and brought them out to observe them. The hard outer shells looked like they would take some cracking to get them open.

BARRET'S CHRISTMAS PARTY

The Barrett's Christmas Party started at the Opera Bar at Circular Quay. Mark usually went there after work on a Friday to wind down and talk through the week's cases with colleagues. He said it was a better idea than bringing it all home and Amy had to agree. It seemed that the whole of Sydney was suing someone. The rate with which litigation had got such a hold on the city was alarming. She'd grown up in an inner city suburb where the neighbours still knocked on your door to borrow sugar. Now, the neighbour was never seen and privacy was expected. Mark would have his usual beers and then head home for the meal she had bought at the food hall near work. She'd decided that a quiet time on a Friday was a better solution than the mass of workers who lined the bars of Circular Quay, with the pushing and the shouting over each other. She didn't think anything meaningful was really discussed, more like an explosion of hot air that needed to be released.

The plan was to meet everyone and their partners for a few drinks and then catch the ferry across the harbour to Neutral Bay. The Barretts had a four storey mansion stretching down the cliff face onto the edge of the water. Tropical gardens lined the path beside the house. They wound down through terraces designed by a leading landscape architect whom Mark's firm had represented in a ferocious battle against the council. The Barretts were very pleased with the way Mark had fought the case. What might have cost them a lot of money, paid for the infinity pool instead. Now the firm was invited there to celebrate and Mark was excited at being regarded as the hero of the moment. It wasn't easy to beat the council with its increasing environmental controls. But Mark had found a loophole that allowed the Barretts to build right to the edge of one of the most beautiful harbours in the world. What was going to be a walking track for the public had become reclaimed by the Barretts as their own private fortress.

Their party group caught the ferry together. Mark had told Amy about how some couples were having problems and she wondered which ones he had been speaking about. He'd also said in a trip they had taken down the coast a month before, that some of the men at work were having affairs. It was a conversation in the car that had no starting point but somehow he had brought it up. She'd told him that was outrageous and what about their marriage and he said that everyone was doing it. He was quiet then as they drove up the M7 and onto the eastern distributor. Amy had felt some disquiet she had no blueprint for and it wasn't until reflection after Mark had left, that she saw he was sending her a warning. She was so naive in what she thought they had, that it never occurred to her he included himself in the 'everyone'.

The stairs to the top deck of the ferry were crowded. Amy ascended to get a better view of the full moon which sat like a dancing white ball over the sails of the Opera House as the ferry lifted in the swell. It was a night for a party in Sydney and Amy felt the tug of the city to let go and be free. A figure brushed past her and she noticed the sleek black hair of the new secretary. She smiled and continued up the stairs but Amy had felt a strange sensation, a heightened awareness that there had been something more in the contact they'd just had. The emphasis of the contact had felt like a full-stop. She let the thought go but somewhere in the back of her mind, she felt the new secretary had been deliberate in her intimacy. The slow steps she took to the top of the ferry signalled she had all the time in the world to seduce. Now, looking back, Amy realised that she had been sensing the other woman's intent as she marked out her territory.

The tables of white linen and candlelight lined the side of the pool and looked over the passing traffic in the harbour. Ferries, pleasure cruisers and motoring yachts had swung into the mood of Christmas and most were lit up like lanterns, criss-crossing between bays. Music carried over the waters in a rising exuberance as the city let go of the year of hard work and signalled the readiness to enjoy the summer celebrations. Mark and Amy were seated next to the Barretts, who were known among locals as the 'property mafia' of Sydney. With the rising prices bringing in easy wealth, the Barretts had secured and sold many luxury homes and apartments. How their name was on so many contracts, brought suspicion of money under the table, but no-one could prove how real estate was increasingly being divided up between banks and overseas interests and how the Barretts had become surreptitiously known as the go-between.

Sydney was famous for its fireworks and everyone in the party was drawn to the banks of the harbour to watch the display. Beside the main event over the harbour bridge, there were smaller celebrations going off along the inlets which dotted the harbour. The Opera House was lit up in an Aboriginal painting of earthy ochres and the harbour itself mirrored the kaleidoscope of colours that merged into marbling as the ferries chugged by. Mark was standing near Amy and she turned to share the moment. 'It's just so amazingly beautiful. We're lucky to live here.' She reached out to touch him tenderly but instead his eyes shot her a warning.

'You're drinking too much as usual. That's your third champagne. Don't embarrass me with the firm.' His face had become twisted a little and his eyes focused meanly on the glass in her hand.

'I'm just trying to keep up with you.' She'd caught his intent to start a round of argument and was willing to play the scene out, if that was what it took to defend herself.

'Honestly, Amy, sometimes you're disgusting.'

The harbour looked cold now, with the moon a washed out glow. She could feel the champagne and the other drinks at the Opera Bar freezing her veins into submission. 'Whatever you say, Mr Gloom and Doom. I'll switch to soda water instead.' She could feel her heart bracing but couldn't make out what the signals were really saying. He turned away from her then to speak to John Barrett and together they huddled by the spa. They looked her way and she thought maybe Mark was warning John not to let the waiter fill up her glass. It wasn't necessary. She'd made a kind of promise. 'Not that he keeps a similar promise to himself,' she thought.

It was when John Barrett joined her and kept her in conversation about land values, that Amy saw Sarah reach out for Mark to dance with her. 'You know, Amy, that husband of yours is worth his weight in gold.' John was smiling the Janus smile she'd seen waft across the party as they arrived. His was a studied ritual, skilled in repaying the firm which had won him such priceless real estate. Bottles of Grange, tickets to the opera and tonight's feast of fresh seafood and French Champagne were his flair of indulgences for anyone he considered on his payroll. He'd also hired the entertainment and Amy watched with unease as girls in gold bikinis circulated in rhythmic dance moves through the crowd.

'That's a lovely bag you have there, Amy.'

It was John's wife this time. Amy caught a collusion between them to keep her occupied. She wondered what she had to offer that could interest the Barretts. Her status at Goldworth and Finch wasn't a reliable source of investigation, as she was part of a team that was directly answerable to the compliance department. There would be no tip offs to the Barretts about which stocks were undervalued and ready to rise. She was placed discreetly between the two hosts and in the social chit chat she had the certainty of being outflanked. It wasn't until later that she realised they were paying their dues to Mark. The Barretts were giving him the space to indulge in any way he pleased by diverting her attention and her ability to move away. Sarah was his pleasure for the night and at this stage Amy had no idea that she'd be going home alone.

Her loose fitting black dress masked her inhibitions as she watched Sarah dancing the Salsa with Mark. The shimmering turquoise dress Sarah wore curved around her body in waves as she moved. Mark's eyes were alight, mirroring the flaming torches along the garden's edge. The music changed to nostalgia and the

80's hit by the Pointer Sisters, 'I'm So Excited,' was played. Amy watched Mark and Sarah move closer with the driving rhythm. Their bodies gyrated together as Amy started to back into the shadows by the statue of Venus, one of many that framed the pool. The repetitive desire of the chorus and its thumping beat nauseated Amy and she excused herself from the Barretts and headed to the bathroom.

'You escaping too, Amy.' It was Janet, the wife of a co-worker from Mark's firm. She was sitting on a bench hugging her knees, the champagne glass beside her nearly empty. 'I couldn't watch anymore. It's like I don't exist. Brad will hardly talk to me.'

Amy could see something in her eyes that looked like terror. She looked like she wanted to escape, to get out of the Barrett's place and just go home. 'You know Brad didn't come home last Friday night.' She was crying now and Amy heard a deep gulping as she tried to suppress the inevitable.

'Are you OK?' Amy didn't know how to help really. Women were left to rot when it came to dismissal. Janet must have been one of the wives whose husband had been having an affair; her mascara was escaping down her cheeks in response.

'He said that he had locked himself in the stairwell at the office. That he'd left his phone inside and couldn't call. I asked him how he got out eventually and he said that he worked out a way to take the door off the hinges. Do you know I actually felt sorry for him!' There was a pathetic stare of resignation. Amy found herself wanting to back away even though she knew she had to offer some sort of support.

'You'll work this out. I'm sure your marriage is secure. Maybe he's having troubles at work and can't tell you about it.' Amy thought maybe he had a gambling problem or something but there was also a girl to girl understanding that she was not long for the discard pile. 'Maybe get yourself a good lawyer just in case,' Amy suggested.

'He is one,' she sobbed and Amy saw in that moment Janet

didn't stand a chance and neither did she.

Outside, the Macarena was snaking through the garden and around the pool. Amy was caught and dragged into a line that exploded at the end of the song into Heavy Metal. The group went wild in orgiastic dancing. She wanted to sit down but Mark's colleague Barry Delany, grabbed her hands and dragged her into the mosh pit. It was in the moment that she saw Mark and reached out to him, that the beat shifted and she was in the water instead. She'd felt the certain push and saw the turquoise shimmer too late to correct the fall. The dancers surrounded the pool and in abandon, others started leaping in as well. Sodden and embarrassed, Amy watched from the water as Sarah led Mark into the garden and up the side path out of sight.

Joan Barrett dressed Amy in designer active wear and called a taxi to take her home. 'Darling, I'm John's fourth wife, you understand.' Amy understood then the female bargain that this was the last night she would see her husband, as a married woman. Somewhere among the ferns and tropical pools outside the cabana on the estate, Mark and Sarah were already hot into their seduction of each other. On the lips of Joan Barrett, 'Darling' held an ache that was the only real thing Amy had left

Through the cab ride home she replayed the loneliness she had been denying for months. The streets of Sydney, lit up again by fireworks overhead, held a macabre dance of light and sound that threatened to make her sick.

'Pull over here. I'll walk the rest of the way.'

It was a full moon with lovers under it somewhere but the steps to her apartment sounded cold and empty. The key to the door was buried deep inside her bag with the ramshackle necessities of lipsticks, cards and receipts in a tangled mess. She fumbled to find it, with the tears flowing freely now. She then looked sideways, distracted by a groaning in the bushes and then a giggling.

'God, Harry there's someone there.'

'Piss off, Lady.'

Then more giggles and a threatening stare from the young man to get out of his territory and leave them alone.

Inside the apartment, the photograph of Mark and her on the bedside table looked innocent. She held it up to the lamp to deliver some sort of understanding. There were few other shots that held their hopes like this one taken before their marriage. Mark had just finished his law degree, which she'd helped finance. They were celebrating with ice-cream. Their bare legs dangled over rocks into the water at the edge of the harbour. They were poor then and had no sense of the trajectory possible in a city and a lifestyle ripe for temptation. She saw the sunburn and the melting cone and then as if in a creeping recognition which had taken years to arrive, she noticed for the first time a luxury cruiser to the side of the shot outside of her focus. A woman in a black bikini was lying over the bow, like a siren. Then Amy noticed where Mark's gaze was drawn, past Amy's smile and onto the distant flirtation.

CINDERELLA DREAM

The sounds of the forest were brought inside to the fire in their first attempts to make sense of why they'd come to The Retreat. Sergio had started a drumming and they were invited to join in. Amy had brought along pieces of sticks that she intended to break and make a cracking sound with. She hoped Sergio and Beth would be kind in their response to the pain the sound had brought up between Mark and herself. She'd been walking along the path to the hilltop above the waterhole, when she realised that the sound of splintering sticks under her feet made her listen more intently.

'You're pathetic, you know that?' Mark's last words had torn into her when he'd come home to retrieve his gear before moving out for good.

'I just don't understand what's happening, Mark. Tell me where things have gone wrong.' Amy was begging but all he could do was cruelly sneer as he went through the drawers. The snapping of the sticks became the snapping of the openings and closings of all Mark's things as he gathered his life into suitcases and into his BMW parked outside. The guilt he had in the excitement he was going to had become twisted into a loathing for the wife he was ready to let go.

'You know what, Amy, you just don't get it. I'm over you … your whining, your drinking.'

'What about you, Mark? Can't you see the same?'

He stopped then and looked around as if the room had suddenly become too small for him. 'You'll need to be out within a month. I've made a date with the tribunal to sort out the rest.'

She scanned the empty drawers of their life together and in the back of a shared cupboard, she was left with a jumper she'd knitted for him. Amy found herself breathing in his smell before it left her forever. She remembered holding it to her chest, as the distance between the road he was on and her arms, played out to nothing.

The music shifted as Eileen, the older woman on the retreat, joined in with a sound blown through a hole in a large seed. There was a howling spookiness which she caught in the playing and Amy wondered what the layers were that she was trying to communicate. She was playing as if there was no-one else in the room. Her greying hair hung to her shoulders and she seemed to hide behind the fall of it. Hers was a world that had been locked away and Amy sensed a kindred spirit. She thought that perhaps this woman was ready to let go of something that she could not do in the outside world. Maybe the retreat might open up a doorway she could escape from into something better.

The whole experience had lasted about five minutes and Amy wondered why Liam had not even attended. She felt guilty that she hadn't been more communicative when they'd met by the river. It was her usual hesitancy to connect, she knew. She'd turned back as she walked away from Liam and saw how he had started to wade into the water, shoes off and jeans rolled up. There was something in the way he walked that reminded her of how she held her body, arms folded like it was cocooned. 'Some way to protect the self from the shocks that just keep coming,' she thought.

She'd lost that early confidence of her twenties when she could easily dissolve the barriers between a man she liked and herself. Mark and she were free with each other before marriage. He'd even called her, 'his wild amore' but life inside a corporate box had clipped her wings too suddenly. Entrenched patterns of life had started to surface with no maturity to call on and as their relationship started to be tested, it all fell apart.

'Are you OK, Amy?' The music had stopped and Beth was touching Amy's shoulder.

'I'm sorry, I didn't realise I was in such a daze.'

'Don't worry, it happens here. Is there anything you'd like to say?'

'I'd just like to know if I'm safe being here. There are things happening I didn't expect.' She remembered Mark telling her that he could re-shape her body with proper gym work. She was already a size 10 but it never felt enough for him. She remembered being examined in her swimsuit, as if she was part of a display with all the other women on Bondi, and she'd come in last. The time she found herself crying in the change room of DJ's department store while Mark waited impatiently outside, signalled it was either him or her who had the problem with relationship. Now she started thinking it was the both of them. How she had measured herself through his eyes, was failing herself, she was realising.

'I should have just told him to go and get it over with. I wasted so many years because I was afraid.'

'Afraid of what, Amy?' Beth was gentle and Amy noticed Sergio had got up and was out on the veranda. There was only Eileen left to witness.

'Afraid of myself, I guess. Can I cope if there's only me?'

She didn't want the group hug and Beth and Eileen didn't look like that was their intention anyway. Amy had come here because in truth she had nowhere else to go. She'd found herself in a small flat off a busy highway. She'd picked up second hand furniture off eBay but the flat still looked desolate and unloved. One wage couldn't buy the luxury apartment that she was used to with Mark and a weekend away from the reality of closed doors and windows to keep the fumes and noise outside, seemed like a good idea.

'I'm not feeling sorry for myself really, I just don't understand how it ended like this.'

'Maybe this is not an end, Amy. Maybe it's a beginning.'

Beth was sprouting all the psychology Amy had read about in the self-help books she'd got out from the library to help make sense of life. The thing though was not what Beth was saying but how she was saying it. There was some kind of compassion there that Amy hadn't got from co-workers or friends and she thought that Beth was not just here for the money but that she wanted to help.

The Irish woman then spoke. 'You'll survive, Amy, my dear.

The spirit's delicate though.' Eileen was being cryptic but it looked like she was in some kind of battle with herself. Her eyes were alight with resolution but the body gave away a futility, as if the weight of the odds were beyond her. Amy smiled at her and excused herself. She could see the moon over the tree tops and wanted a space to breathe. She could hear the river downstream in a heightened awareness as she left the room and could hear Eileen start to speak behind about a 'lost child' and 'a long time ago.'

The night was starlit. Above, the Milky Way spread across the sky in an intricate dot painting of indigo and white. All those millions of eyes blinking down. She'd closed the broken doorway in suburbia where her dreams were left abandoned and now Amy didn't feel so alone in this wild space which connected with an echo from her past. The ironic emptiness of the city with its traffic jams outside her apartment felt absurd. The population was being crammed into a test tube of poor planning and its effect was an urban nightmare.

The cabins had their fires funnelling in a ring of smokers. Cabin 4 was now occupied and Amy could see the silhouette of a figure, seemingly familiar. Through the window, she could see that he was reading by a lantern. His back was to her but the shape of his big frame looked like the swimmer she'd seen that morning. Again, she was drawn into his space and she found herself standing and staring. 'A bit like a stalker,' she cringed. What was it about this person that had her so enthralled? His solitude was mesmerising to her. In his aloneness, she was seeing the opposite to herself. Instead of the hunched shoulders and the withdrawn countenance, here was someone who had their own silent presence. It was something she felt herself longing for.

Liam was sitting on his front steps as she went by on the way to her cabin. There was a different intensity in the dark about him as if in the shadows he was revealed. 'You didn't want to come tonight?' She tried to make a connection this time but something about Liam made her hesitate.

'Just a bit tired that's all. I didn't have too much to offer so I thought it was best to stay away.'

God, he sounded like her when the black dog was biting. There were many times that she'd stay away from invitations because she didn't think she had the nerve to front up alone. The Retreat was one of the first places she'd actually tried to reach out to. She'd tried with friends but they were busy with work commitments and some with disasters of their own.

'We just said what we felt OK to share.'

Amy felt like she was in role reversal being the one to comfort someone. It wasn't easy seeing a man who seemed to be in a sad state. She was so used to seeing Mark in control that she had forgotten how he'd actually let himself go for a while too and when she had said something about him ironing more than his collar for work, he had turned away resentfully. She also remembered how on his birthday, they'd invited a number of friends who didn't show up. He seemed fine with it and said Pete Brady, his best mate, was away in Bali and couldn't be expected to make it. She had an uneasiness that something wasn't quite right but the pedestal she'd put him on, blinded her to seeing him as a human being with flaws of his own, which other friends were obviously growing tired of. It was only in the firm that his talents were secure really, now that she considered it.

'I thought I might have a swim in the river. Call for help if I'm not back in an hour.' All of a sudden Amy had a strong urge to cleanse herself. She wasn't going to invite Liam and he didn't seem to think it was a good idea anyway.

'Bit cold, don't you think?

'Yes but it's a full moon at Easter and it's a million times better than a shower in a cold city flat.'

The bank of the river was wide and grassy where you could enter. It sloped in gently so Amy had no fear of losing her footing and besides she was a good swimmer. She stripped off and walked in with the intention to swim to the rock on the far side. There wasn't a strong flow and the moonlight was bright, mirroring white onto the water. The cold shocked her though and she questioned whether or not she was being stupid to swim alone and at night. She knew there were logs on the bottom and she'd heard of swimmers being caught in them, so she decided to breast-stroke across and stay on the surface rather than dive under and risk being snagged. Her skin braced and she felt a clamping strength that was needed for survival. How she had missed the signs of Mark not coping, was a mystery she was only just beginning to recognise. She scratched her knees as she pulled herself onto the rock platform and hugged herself as she sat there shivering.

'Why don't we invite your parents over sometimes, Mark?'

She could hear herself naively trying to patch up a family that she now saw was broken. The usual excuse was that his dad was away a lot and his mum was too busy with her socialising. She thought it was herself that was the problem. That they were not interested in getting to know Amy. But as she lay on the rock with her face to the night sky, she was beginning to see that they had washed their hands of Mark when she had taken him over. She began to wonder if it had been like that when he was a child. The family photos showed smiling achievement but that was all. No snapshots of everyday life, just the honour roll at school and at college. Amy could see Mark reaching for the bottle and making some kind of display that it was only the best vintage he'd drink but that didn't strike with the reality that it was just as toxic as the family he'd come from.

Amy lay on the rock and the wash of the past memory of a young bride held her in sorrow. They had a chance and destroyed it together or was it that they had no chance really because of who they were and where they'd come from? Mark with a family who were distant and her with a family who still lay in shadows away from perception. Where had the self-deprecation come from? The woman who couldn't argue for the case to be heard and who had rolled over so easily? Maybe the distance between her family members meant even more souls were tucked away in broken dreams. Maybe purgatory existed after all. Maybe that's just how life is.

Amy saw again the woman in white who stood by her young bride's bed that night. The woman who called to Amy to see the reality of a Cinderella dream. There was no Prince Charming and no glass slipper. Just a boy and a girl staring out into a night sky without a sextant. The figure danced between the trees in the moonlight, Amy not able to distinguish between the light surrounding the woman or Amy's longing for her. She watched as the figure faded away behind a cloud and then Amy began to really weep for the first time since Mark left.

HONEYMOON IN FLORENCE

Their honeymoon was near the Ponte Vecchio in Florence. The olive and cypress trees grew in pots in the courtyard of the villa. Mark had bought her sunflowers for the blue vase on the table but also had stocked the bar with a selection of Italy's finest wines for himself. The black rooster symbol of the Chianti Classico bottle was positioned on the table near the pool.

Amy remembered floating on her back in the pool in the black costume she'd bought especially for its revealing neckline and slimming shape. The Duomo rose up like a bishop's hat on the skyline, the beginning of the Renaissance a timeless aspiration she hoped to discover in her desire to come to Italy.

'It's so beautiful, Mark.'

'Mm, not bad.'

He had already opened the wine and had quaffed half the bottle. Standing on the edge of the terrace, with glass in hand, he seemed more distracted by his own thoughts than the architecture or the invitation of his new wife. It was a hot summer's evening. Amy dived deeply below the waterline to disguise the tears that were already starting to form. She surfaced then and swam to the side, noting he hadn't yet looked her way. Mark was onto the rest of the bottle as she pulled the towel around her to join him.

'You didn't want to swim then? Not like you.' Amy was reluctant to recognise the signs of neglect on that first night after the long flight from Sydney. She'd seen the attractive flight attendant he'd paid attention to for most of the trip though, but excused it as Mark exercising his charm.

'You can't do laps in a pool like that. I'm not into tea bagging. But you go ahead.' She could see how he held the glass steady in his hand to cover the gap between them. The week was already starting to appear drawn out. How was she to know that he had resolved to settle into his usual routine, as soon as he could work out how to access life beyond the confines of the villa?

'I thought perhaps you'd want to come in and just be together. It's a warm summer's evening and we're in Florence after all.' Amy recognised the pleading tone of the vanquished which she had known would build if she didn't stop and correct herself. So she had conceded to the half glass left in the bottle which he began to pour for her.

Outside the villa, in an apartment on street level, the sound of an operatic voice in ascending and descending scales could be heard. Mark had become agitated as the vocal coach stopped his piano accompaniment to instruct the young man whom Amy could see standing in profile by the window. 'God, of all the luck we have to listen to that. Perhaps you should have done your homework before booking, Amy. How am I meant to sleep with a cat's wail?' His words still echoed through time to accuse her.

Amy had found herself praying the music would stop even though she recalled the sound of it had brought a longing in her that still made her sad. Something in the singer's voice had connected to her, unlike her marriage which had already begun to break apart. Nearby was her husband who had begun pacing in frustration as she took too long to dress for dinner at the bar he'd selected, the new red cocktail dress she'd been saving for him not given a second glance.

'Well, I hope they've stopped by the time we come back, that's all I can say.'

She remembered glimpsing his way as he preened himself at the mirror, fixing his collar and primping his hair. There was an exclusive look which he gave to himself that Amy had never seen given to her. But to admit the truth of it was too much for her to contemplate back then.

'So, where are we going to eat, Mark?' She remembered how she had already given Mark the position of command in the hope that that would make him happy.

'I thought tapas at the bar near the bridge would be good.' Amy remembered how her dreams of a candlelit Italian restaurant were shelved. Mark wanted Negronis as an aperitif, the precursor to several cocktails later. She knew she'd be lucky to order a gourmet Panini, if that.

The club filled with tourists and locals had the familiar look of patrons in the bars back home in Sydney. The memory of squashed body contact being mandatory, made her feel like she was in on a conspiracy which she was not privy to. Amy could see that no-one was really talking to each other as their eyes danced across the scene to pick out a new desire. There was a mutual acceptance that it was a place to be seen, not a place for a honeymoon couple at all. Mark was enthralled. She remembered how men seemed just as much interested in each other and when one particular dark Italian pressed against Mark, Amy had replied with jealousy.

'Can we just leave? It's stuffy in here.' She was smaller than most of the patrons who looked over her head and past her but Mark had stature and the buff of a gym goer. Amy saw there were many who were drawn to his Aussie accent and good looks.

'Look, Amy, if you don't like it why don't I meet you back at the villa later. I'll just stay for a few more drinks.' Amy recalled how her naive belief masked the reality. It would be well into the early morning when Mark arrived home to sleep on the couch.

That first night in the Villa Fiorenze was a disaster for a honeymoon. Yet Amy had hoped Mark would consent to walk around the heart of the city to the galleries Uffizi and Accademia, even if that walk was behind dark glasses to cover the extremes of the night before. Michelangelo's David had stood in marble, the nude form the perfect male, she had thought. She saw the rock that was held gently but securely in David's hand. She had thought of Mark holding that rock to protect her, dreaming of a future security together. But at Uffizi she had also watched and saw him again looking at the women moving around the gallery. Feasting on dark Italian eyes and olive skin. The curve of their hips in the swish of their skirts.

One in particular had held him entranced and he even had the expectation that Amy would be impressed. 'She looks like one of those paintings, doesn't she? She has that mysterious look.' He had pointed to the Titian painting of Flora the Goddess of Spring. The idealized woman, bare breasted with the offering of flowers. A sensuality out of reach to him just as David's strength was out of reach to her. His admiration sparked a warning note again. If he was enamoured on their honeymoon by strangers as he had been the night before, what was the real future for them? And so she bit.

'I can see a person who has to get up at six and go to work. I can't see too much difference between us. I think you're putting her on a pedestal, like David.' Amy had been playfully provocative, she recalled, but the depth of his antagonistic response had stunned her.

'God, Amy, you haven't got much subtlety have you?'

And that was it. One comment about a woman he liked and she had been a pariah for the rest of the trip. She had even found herself eating pasta alone in the Palazzo Vecchio, scoffing down the local wine in an attempt to dull the fact that her new husband had decided to go jogging without her. The touch of their love making had become coarser. She still hoped that surely a few words of disagreement could be resolved. But it took two people to want to try and back home in Sydney she started to find that Mark's early leaving and late return from work was more than just 'trying to get ahead'. Even on weekends he was constantly out with his mates and the loneliness she had felt, left little of Amy intact to see the obvious.

That night at the retreat, Amy recalled how one of the last images of Florence was of an old man feeding birds, holding bread out with a gentle hand. She had gone alone to the Ponte Vecchio to buy the gold ring that Mark had promised her but had forgotten to purchase. The old man was quietly present to the birds and not to himself at all. She'd watched as he bent in supplication, the birds in turn waiting for their time to peck at the crumbs he was offering. She had tip-toed past the man in concentration and found the address on the card. Inside the small workshop, a master goldsmith sat at his table, his long black hair flowing freely as he worked like an alchemist and artist combined. He had told her that the ring she was to buy was a story of the stirring of the soul. Then he'd held it gently in his hands as he waited for her reply.

'Grazie, è bellissimo.'

He had smiled at her then and she understood the ring would be a secret she would keep.

'Arrivederci signora.' This quiet moment of Florence was hers alone. She wished she'd taken the time back then to look for more.

LETTING GO

Early morning and she woke bereft. Something had shifted overnight and she felt herself shedding a skin, like a snake. Mark was just one piece of the puzzle, she felt sure of that. The sense of liberation that she had hoped for in her early love with Mark, was a façade for a deeper malaise, she knew. She was feeling a pain that held some kind of answer to her life so far. She hoped the day of discovery would reveal more of the questions that were beginning to arise. She'd seen the woman in white like a ghost figure in the night and felt that somehow she might be a key to unlock the puzzle. Her past doubts of her worthiness as a wife and her ability to manage a job which was becoming increasingly questionable, all rose to a scrutiny that she seemed ready to face. What was it about Amy that called for a drink each time the fear surfaced, that pushed her further away from herself?

The task for today was to draw. Again nothing explicit. The team at the retreat seemed to have a trust in something beyond themselves which was working on them as well as the participants. Amy had heard of eco-therapy or green therapy coming out of San Francisco but decided they'd all been connected to the land throughout history anyway, before New Age thinking came along. The rebirth and spring harvest of the Easter Festival was a dying and a rising up again, she considered. How many times had her dreams died? She was not alone in that question when she walked the city blocks with the rushing crowds with their heads down. The speeding trains with headphone speak, into worlds without conversation. From the beginning the yearning was there to climb higher in the tree outside her front door. The little girl with the fierce force denied. Some answer in life was calling her out. All she had to understand was the question she'd been sent here to find.

She picked up the gumnuts she'd put in her pocket the day before and thought the hard outer shell was there to protect some beginnings of life inside. To think it could grow into the enormous flowering gum that lined river banks across Australia. Amy knew her drawing of it couldn't bring out that reality and resolved to take them back to her flat in Sydney. She'd put them on the windowsill as a reminder that some places things grew without restraint, unlike Sydney where apartments and crowded high-rise were taking the place of beautiful old buildings, which held a historical link to the architecture of the past. Who wanted a city that was just concrete, glass and steel? Thank God the green bans of the 1960's and 70's preserved The Rocks area but even that was being eroded now with older residents being moved out to make way for 'progress' along the harbour. Trees had been poisoned to get a water view before the council could stop those individuals and commercial interests who felt they had a right to carve up Sydney, as if was their own to play with.

'You don't think there's an irony in you sending emails to the mayor about the trees when you're a share trader who rips people off every day?'

Mark had that look of, 'You're such a hypocrite,' that she had seen many times when she tried to have an environmental conscience as well as being paid for the economics degree she'd taken at Sydney Uni.

'It's a complicated world, Mark. You'd know that with the cases you file. We're all selling our soul in some way. I'm just trying to minimise the effect.' She remembered how she'd climbed every kerbside tree in her street. How she'd lie in bed at night and count the ones she had left. The trees with the higher branches that would need a lift to reach into. The kids on the block who built a ladder out of planks from their dads' sheds to scramble up. The tree-house built from the planks to rest on. This was the world she'd left behind, that she could not enter into again. A world that had lost its childhood and its dreams.

Mark was cold in his reply. He'd forgotten his first dreams or maybe he'd never really had them. 'We all sold our soul a long time ago and there's no turning back. All we can do now is survive and take what you can, when you can. That's my motto and it's buying the car we drive, so get over it Amy.' He took what he could before it was too late for him and now the reverberations of that cynicism had her thinking that maybe they were becoming the robots that Jack Mundey and his Green Ban movement had warned about. Maybe they'd grown so far into a world of make believe that what was real didn't exist and if that was real, maybe they were ceasing to exist too.

The top of the hill overlooking the river was lined with yellowing poplars planted long ago as a wind break. Burning red maples were in autumn blaze. Amy decided that here among the fallen leaves was where she could draw her ideas. The path she'd taken to get to the top had been shaped by someone who had placed river rocks as stepping stones. It led out of the bush onto a wide view across the valley where the river was winding sleepily below. The floods had gone and now the river was slowly moving to the delta and out to sea.

The Retreat lay on the bank of one of the curves of the river. On a further curve downstream she could make out what looked like an abandoned house and wondered what story lay there amongst its solitude. A house of 'forget-me-not,' she considered, waiting for a return. She could see the water hole she had swum in last night and wondered what had led her to take that risk, what return she hoped to discover. She considered that the figure in white was an illusion but nevertheless it was the second time she'd experienced some kind of connection outside herself that had come at a crossroads in her life. How life held warnings as well as promises, she'd come to accept, but finding how to live was a difficult balancing act she had kept getting wrong until now.

The gardens encircling the cabins and main house below had patchworks of crop rotations and fruit orchards. It looked like a giant eye and as she sketched, she tried to capture the spiralling energy of the design which complemented the river winding through the valley. A natural flow emerged and she thought it wasn't the picture that mattered so much but what was happening in the expression of it. She thought about the stories of the bush and how Aboriginal people had danced to bring the spirit back into the land and themselves. The souls of their feet pounding the earth in ancient rhythms. She had loved to dance but Mark would refuse to dance with her. 'And yet there was no hesitation in dancing with Sarah,' she thought. She considered that all the times she'd been held to a spot while the music lifted her up to move, was just another way for him to control her. As Amy drew the dancer in pencil flow across the page, she felt the release.

'Who am I?' She spread out on the ground and felt the earth cushioning her. 'Let go, Amy, it's OK to let go.'

She was talking to herself, encouraging something inside to soften. She could see the tops of her toes as she lay flat, with her arms spread wide. Her breath deepened. She tried to locate where the pain was sitting. Every time she tried to capture it, it shifted and lit up areas across her body like a pin-board of pain signals. This is where you had been accused of paranoia when you asked why he was out so late. This is where you'd been told you were 'a piss weak person' when you cried over a relationship you could see crumbling. This is where the face in the mirror believed that what was being said was true.

'He likes women, you know that. All kinds of women.' It was Barry Delany from Mark's firm with his own particular leer. 'We can do a few drinks of our own if you like. I can meet you after five at The Menzies.' Barry had surprised her from behind at a work gathering Mark was absent from, his voice low and cunning in its intent.

Amy had turned to stare into his eyes to restrain him. There was a knowing smirk fuelled by too many beers. She understood why Mark had told her that this guy would soon be sacked. There was no sense of discretion in his approach. He was out for a quick lay and he'd seen her as an easy target or perhaps to get one up on

Mark. Amy felt intimidated by his presumption that she didn't have much option. 'I don't think Mark would appreciate one of his colleagues hitting on his wife.' She tried to sound light-hearted to keep away any intimacy but Barry was on a different trajectory altogether.

'I know what your husband's been up to and it's not just women I'm talking about. You can tell him from me that if he wants me out of the business, I'll have a few things to say first which he may not like.'

She wondered what knowledge Barry had that threatened Mark's place in the firm and that also allowed him to think he had rights over her as Mark's wife. When she told Mark later that Barry was being suggestive and practically accusing him of something criminal, Mark just shrugged and said, 'He's taking a risk.' Amy thought it was Mark's usual cool demeanour but she could see underneath he'd been disturbed. So, she thought, there was more to Mark and his behaviours than just Sarah the secretary!

How life was about to change. She saw him in the stand of mountain ash, carrying and placing the rocks firmly in place as he built steps up to a lookout. It was the swimmer from the first night, the man in Cabin 4. Amy watched while the pile of rocks he'd brought up from the river was distributed up the slope, winding through the tree line to the top. His was a steady rhythm and effective for the load he was carrying. This time, she wasn't going to let her usual hesitancy win over. She was going to introduce herself and find out who this stranger was and why his presence affected her so much. She left the hilltop clearing and walked into the forest where she had seen him in the distance. The mountain ash were tall with grey furling bark which lay on the track as it peeled and fell away. It was funny but she didn't feel dwarfed by such big trees and as she moved up the path to the top, she began to feel at home here.

She was out of breath when she made it to the top, the final ascent taking on a much steeper gradient near the end. Here the rocks were covered in moss. Fungi grew on the branches and bark that lay around. The stranger was building something out of rocks as she approached. She watched for a moment as he lifted the heavy rock and gently placed it for a seat he was building. She saw someone who wasn't the kind of man from the city that she was used to. His were not the refined movements of Mark, a practised refinement that hid a rougher core, she thought. This man's hands were used to physical labour. They were honest hands. Hands that built rather than tore down. Hands she wouldn't mind touching her.

It was the second time she had noticed how this man's presence moved her. With Mark, she'd been burnt so badly, she couldn't now tell what was real any more. Maybe it was the isolation of the hilltop and he was picked out in broad profile. Maybe it was the forest that was softening her approach. Maybe the yearning inside was her own seed of life crying out for more. Whatever the urge was to get to know this stranger, it was a surprise she hadn't seen coming.

She called gently this time to make him aware that she was there. 'Hello, I was wondering if you belong to The Retreat?' He paused for a moment with his back to her. She watched as he seemed to consider her presence, as if he knew she was there all along. 'I saw you swimming in the river but… um…I don't think you saw me.' She felt foolish as if he'd known she'd been watching and now she'd made it to the top of the ridge, he'd know also that she was following him.

He turned slowly, 'So, you're the first to make it up to the peak.' He was inquisitive but his smile was playful. She could feel his eyes examining her, trying to fathom who she really was.

'I'm Amy. I'm here for the weekend.'

'I know who you are.'

His voice was deep and rounded and she found herself melting into its rhythm. 'Be careful, Amy,' she thought. 'Why would a man like this want to know more about me?' She found herself backing up. Her eyes were down and she stood there exposed.

Surely he could see she was damaged. She could hear the put-downs from Mark, 'As if someone would want you, Amy.' Were they just the voices in her own head though, she thought, the voices which had been there all along.

'I'm sorry, but how do you know my name?'

'I read your profile before you came. My name's Dusty. I'm the caretaker here.' His smile was warm now and his eyes lay on her longer than she had expected.

'My profile?'

'I know it sounds a bit business like, I'm sorry. Just your name. I know your name.' He seemed uncertain as if her name meant something more to him than he was revealing. He shifted his focus then, as if as he placed the last rock, something else was being put into place. 'Would you like to sit down?'

She could feel herself being drawn. There was a sudden falling. So sudden in its entirety. They sat together looking over the valley below, like two kids who had climbed to the top of the tree to look out. From this point on the property, you could look east and see the sea in the far distance. The river opened up into a splintering delta and the farmlands down the valley were lush after the rains.

'It's so beautiful here. No wonder you have built this lookout. It's special. Did you create this place, Dusty?' She was probing, trying to find doors to enter into a conversation that held a promise of return.

'Well, I guess you can say it created me. I came up into the valley to camp and it felt like home. It's a long story but what I've built here was started by someone else. I'm just finishing the job.' He was wistful in his reply and Amy could see him staring into a world she could only guess at.

'When I saw you swimming in the water hole, did you see the platypus?' She tried to focus the conversation into a territory he might be interested in. She'd gone down to the river to see the wild animal with the furry body and the duck-like beak. Its existence a paradox. She felt an irony that here in the wilderness she was finding the company she craved so much back in the city.

'If you swim, they hide. You have to be there really early to catch them or just on dusk. I can show you if you like, later on this evening.' There was something more, she was sure of that. Something that he wanted as much as her but whether it was for the same reason was a question. She resolved to go to the water and see.

'I'd like that.' It all seemed so natural. Here was a man who was part of the retreat and yet she was allowing him to get under her skin so quickly. Where were her defences? Where were the years of not knowing the true intentions of her own husband who lived conveniently without commitment until it was too late? There was also this niggling feeling however, that he was just being polite. She'd be here a few days and then gone. What could she expect from getting to know someone who knew more about her from her profile than she did about him? Someone who would be welcoming the next round of visitors after she'd gone. Her mind wasn't prepared to open up so readily to a stranger but in the freedom of the valley, her body had already begun abandoning any restraint.

'The Flowering of Amy' had been a book she'd owned as a child, given to her by her mother. Her name meant 'Beloved'. The little girl in the book had gathered flowers to wear in her hair and the dress she wore was covered in yellow petals. Amy had loved the book and kept it as an adult until it was lost in one of their moves up the social ladder of the city. Mark had decried a grown up with a fantasy and she suspected the book's spine lay broken at the bottom of some skip-bin he'd hired.

Not wanting children of his own was a further restriction on reality as he saw it. She'd agreed, to please him. The decision not necessary for a hip couple on the move. There was only his way, unless the real Amy stood up. The memories had once stirred in her of a child in a book who played in a garden of dreams. Each seed the young Amy planted there, ready to flower in the spring. A marriage soon wilted though when her begging for a child went unanswered. 'You're selfish, you know that. It's all about you. You don't have the patience to be a mother anyway.' So easy to pull down a dream. His intention, to tie her hands to his desire, mirrored the denial which masked her pain.

She'd let go of her dreams of a family into a winter that lasted. The blinkered regret though, she had kept to herself, when the world around was blooming. There was no other way for a woman tied to a promise to respond, she believed. But now there was a possibility she had left on the hilltop, where a man with a mission had stirred her. A possibility only. But that possibility had already begun to loosen the knots. The stubborn thread, she hoped, was just a push away into freedom.

WOMAN IN WHITE

The walk back down from the peak led Amy on the stone steps through the forest of tall ash and into pockets of rainforest. She'd left Dusty to continue his work and made her way with an easing childlike step. Her senses were opening up, merging into the vegetation as a natural part of it all. The greens became more intense and even the small birds didn't shift from the path as she approached. Sitting on a rock, she started to sketch the epiphytes as they climbed towards the light, their roots clinging to branches of their host and free-falling into the air. The palms and tree ferns held a dappled light and instead of trying to capture the exactness of their form she worked the pencil to find line and form in an abstract way. It was a conversation with the surroundings and as she drew, the intensity of the hidden voices became more observable.

'What's the use? You may as well give up before you start and save yourself the trouble.' It was as if she was drawing the words of her childhood. Some defeat which had happened a long time ago, that had stuck with her until now in a place she felt safe enough to hear it. 'Amy, you have to know your place and accept the way things are.' She understood the acceptance idea but wasn't sure if her place was where she wanted to be or where someone else had put her. It felt like she had spent a lifetime being beaten back into submission. Maybe because she was a girl. Maybe because of the competition to be on top and there could only be one winner.

She remembered escaping to the rooftops, while other kids in the neighbourhood left to play without her. It was like she was trying to say, 'This is me,' but the words became blurred until they were buried deep inside and the 'Me' which was acceptable to others started to emerge. The problem was it was never going to work with a false identity to relate to. The desire, that had started to awaken on the mountain top with Dusty, had a place to grow if she could accept that she was worth taking a chance on. But it wasn't Dusty who Amy needed to convince. She had begun to realise it was herself.

She saw her then amongst the fernery. The woman was sitting in a patch of sunlight that came down between the trees in an opening from the top. This time she was peaceful and Amy didn't feel afraid in her presence at all. There was some connection between who the woman was, and who Amy felt she herself needed to be. Amy knew she wasn't real, that she was some part of her imagination. Maybe an imaginary friend from childhood who had grown alongside her. But she also had a sense she was beyond that, that she had been there before, a woman through time who'd been there to witness and guide. Amy didn't feel the need to try and communicate but to simply observe her presence. What she did feel was a decision that she'd never go back to the person she had been: the woman who Mark had belittled with neglect. Something had been planted in the forest. Something she could nurture now on the outside.

When she came out onto the flats, Liam and Eileen were sitting together by the curve of the river. She stood back at the edge of the forest and watched them for some time. They looked comfortable in each other's space as they sketched the scene of the river and forest beyond. Amy observed the way they both leant into each other like teacher and pupil. Liam positioned his hand for perspective and Eileen immediately responded with committing to paper. It was if they were on their own relationship agenda and not the individual challenge to discover something in oneself.

Amy was still trying to decipher her experience with Dusty. They'd spoken about the property to start with and how he had envisioned a place where people could come to refresh themselves. He said he owed it to people to help them discover and connect with something real that would help to keep them sane. It sounded like he was speaking from experience and she tried to resolve where his motivation was coming from. They'd spoken for about an hour while he kept building around the viewing seat over the valley and then they had sat closely together and she felt like they were the only people in the world. He seemed content to sit with her alone. She hadn't felt that interest from someone in a very long time.

She worked her way through long grass towards the pair who remained engrossed in their work together. It was the second time that day she was to enter into another's reality uninvited. She questioned her own isolating ways that in the past had led her to discover even more loneliness at its core. How was it that some people drifted together so readily and what she needed instead was a battering ram? Time with Mark had diminished her but her new time with Dusty held a promise of bringing an older truth of Amy back. She resolved to find out. 'Hi there. Um, I hope I'm not disturbing you.'

The uncertainty to interrupt though was still recognisable in the faltering tone as both Liam and Eileen turned to Amy with an exclusivity in their eyes. Their hesitation to turn back into themselves, however, was broken by Eileen. 'No, you're welcome my dear. C'mon now, sit yerself down with us for a moment.' Liam then closed the drawing he'd been working on and Amy saw the cue for a privacy that seemed a particular trait of the man.

He was about her age and looked as uncertain as she was. Amy felt like they might share a common splinter of pain. Something in his past had not been resolved and seemed to sit inside the man in isolation. She understood what it was to carry that spectre of loneliness

'Have you completed your assignment for the morning? I took in a bird's eye view from the top of the ridge up there. It's really lovely if you're willing to climb that far.'

'We're happy with where we are. Aren't we, Eileen?'

'Liam's been giving me drawing lessons. I'm not the best pupil though, I'll say that fer sure.' Amy felt left out but was determined to continue. She'd been given attention on the ridge, now she had to find that same acceptance in herself. Eileen's work was naïve but represented something about the flow of the river in the line. It was a bridge to a conversation she needed.

'I'm sure I can see the fish jumping in there. I like it. Would I be able to see what you've drawn, Liam?' She saw how his hand held over the cover of his work but with a look from Eileen he opened the page to show a representation of the scene, which sat so perfectly in place, it seemed to come alive. 'Wow, I'm really impressed. That's so beautiful.' Liam seemed to blush and she thought he had to be an introvert to have so much talent and not be willing to share it.

Amy noted then that Eileen's eyes were red and she looked to have been crying. They didn't ask Amy about what she had drawn and again she felt left out. Amy yearned to be back on that seat way up in the clouds with a man she had met for a moment. She yearned to recapture that touch of suggestion, that she had held meaning for someone. That her existence mattered. She longed for the evening when they were to meet by the waterhole. If even for a few moments, she intended to hold onto that intimacy she hadn't experienced like that before. Then Amy realised that she hadn't stopped to ask Eileen why she looked so sad.

EILEEN AND DAVID

As her cotton dress fell to the ground, all she could hear were the promises. The promises that he'd stay, no matter what the consequence of war. He'd come back and be hers, and she would be his. Forever.

He'd come into David Jones department store where Eileen was waiting behind the counter, his soldier's uniform alien amongst the waft of feminine fragrances. She was just a few weeks off the boat from Dublin and he was the first Australian man who'd caught her eye. She smiled as he picked up bottles of perfume to inspect, putting them down again indiscriminately. It wasn't just the purchase he was here for in the end. He'd seen the girl with the curly hair through the window. It was a simple thing to say hello when buying a present for his mother.

'How may I help ye, Sir?'

'Um, I'm looking for a present for my mother.'

Eileen lifted her eyes to meet his. It was a knowing conversation. One she'd never dared before. But something in the quiet exchange was enough for them both. Enough to close the lonely door of a girl so far from home and open a door for a boy who was being sent off to war.

'Sure, all women like perfume.'

'Well, what do you advise?'

'I think she will like Channel No 5. Most women do.'

'I think she will like you.'

He didn't have the proper time for courtship with his plane leaving for Vietnam soon. She'd seen many young men in uniform lately. They gathered in hotel bars until emptying with deployment. Then the girls who'd seen them off went silent too, waiting for news or for some, moving on.

Now she was holding the young soldier's hand as they took the ferry to Manly, to the little flat she'd rented on a budget. A piano player was playing 'My Girl' as they boarded, some of the passengers already in a singalong as the vessel pulled away from the dock. Eileen could hear someone talking about a big swell out to sea which they'd hit when they went across The Heads.

'Will it be alright, d'ye think?'

'Don't worry. I can swim to save you.'

She felt certain that he meant it.

It was mid-July and cold outside the ferry. They watched across the harbour towards Luna Park which turned into a playground of light at dusk. The giant clown face at the entrance seemed ominous though. Its teeth looked like they could crush in one bite.

'Look, the moon's coming up!' He'd put his jacket across her shoulders as they sat quietly on the bottom outside deck. The orange beacon, rising between The Heads, illuminated the way to Manly.

'It's big alright. Must be a southerly swell. I might need to hold you tight, if that's OK with you?'

Most of the people had already gone inside the ferry when the first swell hit. The bow dug in and rose high before crashing into the one behind.

'I don't like this. I truly can't swim.'

'Don't worry. I'm here to protect you. You would've had to have gone home through this sea tonight anyway. Good thing we met.' He was smiling as he pulled her towards him.

'I don't know yer name.'

'It's David and you're Eileen.' She gave him an inquisitive look. 'Your badge. I couldn't help but notice.' His grin suggested there was more he was looking at besides the name badge on her chest as she'd gift wrapped the present.

The boat was rocking now as the ferry turned across The Heads and took the full swell to its starboard side where they were sitting.

'I think it's safer if we move in.' Her footing was unsure as he opened the door for her and they stumbled inside. Passengers were sitting stoically as the next series of waves hit. She wished they'd turn around and head back to safer waters but the boat ploughed through, across the gap between Watson's Bay and Manly. Outside The Heads, the open sea was a boiling pot. Eileen imagined the engines shutting down, them being helpless in the onslaught.

The musician had been quiet for a while but got back up again to answer a request, the gentle lull of 'Moonlight Sonata' in contrast to the wild seas crashing over the decks. David had found a seat for them in the centre of the boat, away from the windows that now were awash with foam. Eileen couldn't help it, but she was shaking. The music had gone into the frenetic third movement which mirrored the force outside. She was drowning in its rhythms.

'Aw me, will this ever stop?'

'Just go with the music, Eileen. Listen to how he's mastering it.'

In all the clamour, the musician had managed to plant his feet and steady himself, taking each jolt with a determined punctuation of the keys. Eileen could see him close his eyes then and play as if in a trance. The effect caught her by surprise as she watched his sure fingers playing each note deliberately. Then she realised the ferry itself was playing a kind of tune with the seas. Whoever was steering must have known what they were doing too. She imagined she could hear laughter coming from the bridge. It was taking skilful timing, like the pianist, to catch the swell and ride it.

When they reached the dock, Eileen was shivering with some of her outer garments wet. 'Here, keep this jacket on. I don't want you getting sick on our first date.'

'Sure, you don't want to be catchin' a cold either. You'll be needin' a hot shower I think.'

'It depends.'

'On what, might I ask?'

'If you'd join me, I would.'

They walked to the flat slowly. The promenade was lined with pines that seemed to salute as they passed beneath. She was resting her body against his now. He was warm and his voice was tender.

'I think I was meant to meet you.'

'How d' ye mean?'

'It was no accident that I needed perfume for my mother and you were there.'

'Ye think so now?'

'I know so.'

The mirror by the bed reflected the love that had begun that day. His lips were to her cheek, his hands unzipping the jacket he had lent to keep her warm.

The week to follow was all she had to live by but it was more than enough. Each afternoon he was outside her work on Elizabeth Street, roses in his hand. Love wasn't to be counted in time and David had made his promise. 'I'll love you, Eileen, forever.'

She had promised to wait as he left the last time for the plane to Vietnam. It was early morning when he'd kissed her goodbye and late afternoon when he was no longer there to pick her up from work. No-one knew it was Eileen who watched for the letter. No-one saw the young Irish woman standing by the window, with his child in her womb growing. No, no-one knew of her promised love at all.

She had the baby at the women's hospital in the room for the unwed. 'If you don't know who the father is then you can't give him his proper name. Isn't it better for the baby to go to a real family now? One with a mother and a father? Isn't it cruel to keep him when so many families are so desperate?' So, how was she to live? Without her parents and her brothers back on the Shannon, there was no-one to protect her. No-one to say the Hail Mary, for all those sins she'd committed.

She let her son go when the autumn leaves were falling. The bare branches out the window were clutching at the sky. A chill was in the morning the priest arrived to take David from her. She'd chosen the name of his father. David ... the giant slayer. 'Go on now wee lad. Face the giant with yer eyes open and yer back to the sun. 'Cos it'll blind the giant and you, ma darlin' boy, will have the advantage that I can't give to ye.'

So, how could she leave him now? He might be needing her one day. She couldn't return to Ireland to her little home on the river with her father cutting wood to make the furniture. Fine furniture with not a lot of buyers who could afford it.

Her father he would say, 'The world's yer oyster, Eileen. Sure the only soul stopping yerself is you.'

Then her mother she would reply, 'Don't you go putting those innocent ways into her head now. She'll never stop dreaming, and sure what good'll that do her?'

But she had believed her da and had sailed on the ship to Sydney. To see the world. Her father said that she was his little bird to go and bring the stories back. But she had never returned and her mother … well, she was right enough.

Now the hair in the mirror is turning grey. The autumn leaves fall quietly onto the bathroom floor where she sweeps them into a bin. Her boy would be forty this Sunday. 'Easter Sunday when Christ our Saviour will rise again.' She holds on to that promise that each year her David too will go on in life in his son out there somewhere.

She saw him in the playgrounds as she walked the streets of Sydney. She saw him riding the waves at Manly, all bleached hair like his father. She saw him sitting under a tree one day in Hyde Park writing poetry. 'That'll be the Irish blood in him.' But then she realised that she could be wrong and none of those boys and men were her David and she didn't know what he looked like at all. There was no promise that he'd stayed in Sydney. He could be anywhere in the world and she had wasted her time hoping. Then the howl would come in the night like a wolf, that he could be dead like his father. So, she had waited for the days to be over, so the next day could come and the next.

Then, one day a letter came. The mailman brought her an offer for a retreat and she hardly had to pay anything at all. It said she could spend Easter, 'In the valley where the river winds slowly to the sea.' She'd given up her faith such a long time ago. No Easter mass could heal her wound but a retreat was a ritual back home where they would sing the holy songs and think of Jesus and Mary and Joseph and promise to be good, no matter what. So she had decided, 'Sure why not take this chance? Maybe I can feel the Shannon's waters again. Maybe I can wash my sins away so far from home.'

The plane dipped its wing over the round house and gardens and landed on a runway a half hour drive away. The retreat bus passed through fields she could have mistaken for home, all green and plenty. 'I can breathe at last up here, away from the silent city with its lonely walls.' She didn't know how the offer came to her door but she was glad it did and that she had decided to take this chance on luck. The younger woman kept looking out the window and the young man she'd met, who called himself Liam, sketched as they drove. She liked him right away and when he helped her down the stairs, she held on to his arm like he was hers. Forever.

When Eileen entered Cabin 1, she held her breath. Above the fireplace, carved in timber, were the words from back home from an old Irish prayer, 'And until we meet again, May God hold you in the palm of his hand.' She wondered, 'Sure, do they know I've come from the old country, or if it's just coincidence?' She could see her mother sitting in the rocker by the fire, knitting the Aran yarn for the sweaters. The rosary, said by da, would become a thread that wove into a prayer, which spun like the yarn of ma.

She could see the river from her window. 'I'll pretend and call it the Shannon for old times' sake,' she whispered to herself. No-one would know her dreaming ways and how she longed for the familiar. 'Before the ferryman takes me away.' The circular shape of the retreat reminded her of a fairy fort and so she mused, 'Wouldn't that be somethin' now, if the little people were here to greet me? I've been in Australia too long to redeem m'self, but not so long as to forget where I belong.'

Then she rocked and remembered Beckett's play, *Rockaby*,

when she'd gone to the Abbey Theatre. She could see the old woman rocking herself into and out of the light. Or was it that she was being rocked by something else? It was hard to say. But she was deliberate in how she kept saying, 'More.' Like some child asking to be swung higher and stronger, only her rocking was becoming weaker and frailer instead.

It was all confusing but Beth was very nice with her soft eyes and sweet smile. Eileen liked her right away. Beth seemed to give her special consideration when she checked her in and Eileen thought it must be her age. 'Now, you let us know if there's anything we can do for you. The fire's been lit and we hope you find the cabin cosy enough.'

'Well, thank you, m'dear. You're too kind.'

She could hear herself adopting the voice of her mother and regretted, 'Not long now Eileen, if ye haven't crafted yer own voice yet.' She wanted to know if the retreat had prayers and such but Beth just said, the forest and river would be their church for this Easter. Eileen didn't think that sounded blasphemous though, since she was a non-believer anyhow, now that many of the priests had gone off. Tomorrow they were to find music in the trees and she thought, 'Fancy askin' an Irishwoman to find music, when it's right inside in the blood in yer veins. Sure no need to be findin' it now but sharin' it with strangers, well that's another matter.'

ROWAN TREE

The next morning, Eileen made her way up to the hill and looked to the ridge higher up. The mountain ash trees there shared the name of the rowan trees from back home. She knew it as the Traveller's Tree, so those pilgrims on a journey couldn't get lost. Her mother would instruct her how the rowan would protect her from invisible forces and so her mother said she was to keep her wits to the end with its magic in her. She felt, 'This is the right place to be, with the signs of the past here too.'

The trees on the ridge and down into the valley below had been planted in rows and she knew that someone must have been there before to start the new growth. Someone had seen the future in this stand of trees and she wondered who it was who had measured the ground and planted the seeds so long ago. She also wondered who it was who had left the house she could see in the distance to stand so alone and unkempt like a forgotten island.

She wondered why the retreat was built in this valley and was determined to ask Beth when she returned from the project for the day, to find sounds that meant something to her. Sergio's task was a simple request and she thought, 'Sure why not give it a go, and try and remember what brought me here?'

He'd taken her to Luna Park that week, after she'd finished work one day. She carried the roses he'd brought, like a posy. The clown teeth opened to invite them in but each bite of fun, she knew, was one step closer to saying goodbye.

He wanted to show her where he came as a child, when his mum and his dad had brought him down from the country for the Royal Easter Show. All the kids waited for the time, he said, to make their mark in the city with the showing of the livestock and food they had grown. 'City kids don't even know where their food comes from,' he said. 'Wouldn't it be crazy then if they didn't look after the country and the farmers? We'd all starve.' He had that look on his face that said he was worried about this idea. 'I'll show you the country when I return. You will love how big it is but you will also see how fragile it is too.'

Eileen could see what he meant when she looked over the valley with its winding ways. The water was just starting up here but anything that entered it further downstream couldn't be taken back. There'd be no saviour for the water then. No Holy Trinity to piece together a flow that had been damned. She wondered what it would have been like to have been his bride and bring up their son in a valley like this. In the city, the land was forgotten but out here, it seemed like the only real thing that mattered.

David had said he was fighting for his country even though it wasn't their fight really. She questioned why he was going then and he said she sounded just like his mum and dad who had begged him to be a conscientious objector, like his mate from school. But he just said he was prepared to wrestle with fate and take the fight right up to them, like any digger would. He'd said he'd write as soon as the censors let it through, but the letter never came and he had no way of knowing the son he left behind.

Eileen cast a wide net around to see what might be good for making a sound. A kookaburra was laughing in the branches and she thought, 'There's no joke to be had here.' She picked up a seed and tried blowing through it, wondering why it was bare inside, 'Like a hollow heart,' she thought. 'This is what it sounds like to be me. I could blow the music out of me forever, as long as I had the breath to do it.'

'You'll wait for me, Eileen.'

'I'll wait for ye, David... till there's no waitin' left in me to give.'

She could hear the helicopter blades thumping on the TV at night. David down in the jungle with the guerrilla fighting all around. Him on his belly in the mud. The Viet Cong firing over him. Outside her flat, the chanting of, 'Stop the war,' thundered down the street. People with painted white faces would fall and get up and fall again. And Eileen thought, 'Over and over there is no answer, only questions left to hang and fall with the bombs.' So, when the guns went quiet and no word from David came, she knew there'd be no coming back at all.

She continued to retrace the steps they'd taken together through Sydney and their one weekend up the coast before he left for good. He wanted to show her, 'The best surfing spot in the world!' They hired a cabin on Boat Beach and stood on the sand in the early morning light as the fishermen launched their wooden boats and headed out to sea, stroking through the swell with oars instead of motors. 'So as not to disturb the fish,' he grinned and she didn't know whether to believe him or not. Eileen sat on the rocks and cried out that she may lose him when the wave rose up but he launched onto it in one easy pull of the board. David, sliding down the face of that wave, glided over a blue silk stream. That night with the locals at the campfire on the beach, his eyes were alight with a fire Eileen would never forget.

She tried to stay working at David Jones but as her belly swelled the manager said she'd have to go. The management didn't like to see a pregnant woman with a ring on that wasn't hers. Then there was no fight left in her at all. She had stood at the counter and tried to recall the moment he entered and had come over to her with that determined smile. She had imagined it would be possible that he'd come again. But no-one came. And so when they said to leave, she wanted a place where she could not see the people arriving without him.

The convent gave her work but she'd peel the potatoes into a pot down the yard, away from the nuns and their privacy. Then she was kept in a room out the back, with a single bed and a bible beside. 'The wages of sin is death,' it said and she wondered if her love had been cursed from the start. Another poor girl had been there before to help her to know, but all Eileen was left with was a note of regret, lifeless and crumpled under the mattress. 'Too late for salvation for some,' it read. Yet the sound of David's promise held Eileen close to the child as it grew and she tried not to see when the time would come, when a young couple from the parish would arrive to drive her to the hospital. She never met the couple again but after David was taken away, she thought that maybe it was them who waited nearby all the time. Maybe it was that young couple the priest had gone to and promised a child for them at last.

Through the trees at the edge of the rainforest, Eileen could see the woman from the plane who had been introduced last night at the fire as Amy. She watched as Amy bent to pick up sticks and then pause for a while. 'Deep in thought like me,' she supposed. Amy's figure was turning inwards with the bent shoulders and Eileen wondered what had brought her here to the valley. She seemed intent on watching something and it looked like she was speaking to someone Eileen couldn't see. She felt like she shouldn't be staring but something drew Eileen further into Amy's world. She could hear her saying, 'I can't understand,' and then Eileen saw her throw herself on the ground and start to cry. She looked like one of those priests at church who prostrate themselves before the cross. 'There must be something in that if she lies flat out like that too. Down among the leaves.' It wouldn't have been right to disturb her, so Eileen left her there to the thoughts she was wrestling with, trusting that the land could hold her up.

That night at the meeting by the fire with Sergio and Beth, Amy spoke about being afraid. Eileen reached for her hand and the young woman allowed her to hold it for a time while she spoke. Eileen could see how fragile Amy was. A version of her in her youth. A woman in the world without a rudder. It was a world where the symptoms of irrelevance was a sad heart. But somehow Amy had brought herself to admit her fear and in the letting go Eileen saw her strengthen again and relax.

When Beth asked Eileen about her journey, Eileen noticed Amy get up and leave and so she had Beth all to herself to confide in. She told Beth of her little boy and Beth held her attention. It was the first time Eileen had felt anyone truly listen. There was not much to say except he was gone but Eileen had never left him in her heart and mind. She told Beth about her love for her little boy and Beth seemed to be moved by her story. At one point Eileen didn't think Beth could bear to hear her talk about it anymore as she reached for the tissues herself. Eileen then told Beth of his first cries and the way she held him to her chest to keep him warm. She spoke of how the nurse took him to weigh him and he was seven and a half pounds. A good, healthy size.

The nurse had let Eileen hold him for a while longer and then the priest had come. She told how she could hear him slapping down the corridor in his sandals. She had looked to the window and saw the trees fading and cried out to her God, 'Not now, Lord, not now. Dear Lord, please not now.' She could hear the whispers in the corridor and a man's and woman's voice speaking. She could hear a baby crying and a woman's voice shushing. Then she looked to the window and she could see the leaves falling.

Then the doctor came with a needle and she was locked in a dream where she looked through bars to her baby outside. She could hear her boy crying as she reached out to touch him. But she couldn't get near him. She couldn't protect him like the rowan tree could. So she sent her only hope to him, to grow strong wherever he was planted.

LIGHT ON LIAM

Dusty had wanted Liam to report about the mining company that was making access arrangements for mining along the valley floor. Dusty had phoned the paper and asked for Liam personally. Said he was an old school buddy to pretend they were close, so they put him through to Liam's desk. He could hear a quiet anger in Dusty that bore insistence rather than defeat. 'You see the city doesn't get it. They think that food and water is on tap, without effort. It's either clean air and water or our resources going offshore to some absent investor who has no interest in the land or the people. The profit they are after is not for our good, but theirs.' Dusty said that each time in history has its decisive moments and this moment was critical for the farmers and their families, as well as the wildlife that would be displaced forever. Liam knew, however, that in reality the industry wasn't about to lie down for a simple farmer from an unknown valley on the east coast.

'I get it, Dusty. But why me? What have I got to offer that can help you out?'

'I know you will form a connection to this place if you can only come up here and see for yourself. There's something special about this place and there's someone special I want you to meet.' Dusty went on to tell Liam about The Retreat and how he and a man he called Old Jack, had built a place of connections. 'It's all about connecting to the land and the environment and understanding that we need each other. It's all about our humanity and how we co-exist. You see I've made a promise to Old Jack and he's made a promise to the land.' He told Liam that Jack had spent years replanting the trees he had logged. He said he'd made a mistake. He told Dusty that the land was alive and that we needed to heal it to heal ourselves. Dusty had said, 'I just want you to write about it, Liam. Show the way it is out here. How else will people know that what they are giving away, is for nothing worthwhile in the end?' His ideas were simple and Liam didn't want to say how the world has changed and that we live with far more complexity and sophistication now.

'The thing is though, I would like you to take part in the retreat yourself, before you go back to report on it. I'd like you to visit at Easter. It's a beautiful time when the trees change colour. I'd also like you to be my guest. And bring your sketchbook. I saw your artworks on the net and I like the way you have expressed the light.' His enthusiasm for Liam to come held something unfathomable, like a yearning that held them both. Liam thought maybe the connection he was speaking about with the place and with Jack, had already begun to work on him. Liam looked along his desk to the walls of the office. Ladderings of coloured light spilled across the floor, up the wall and onto the ceiling, the glass edges of the louvres bending the light his way.

He had been trying to capture that light since he was a schoolboy in Sydney. He'd try and catch it with his fingers, the flickering up the brick walls of the school and along the corridors, disappearing into shadows as the clouds rolled by. At the beach, he'd find the light in the waves as they curled along tubular and sleek and he'd point his board along its edge. And then he'd search for the light between cracks in buildings. Light, which found words in his poetry that spread and blended into his paintings. Perhaps it was a good idea to chase the light in the country where it was a broad wash.

He hadn't left Sydney since his parents had passed away in a car accident two years before. He'd buried himself into work at the paper, instead of letting the grief come. They'd been kind to him but he felt that part of him was missing, like a hole he couldn't fill. They'd always sensed that yearning in him. Now the axe was coming down on journalists and he knew that no matter how long he stayed at his desk, in the end it wasn't the quality of his work that would keep him employed but the intention of the investors. He knew his grief, in all its layering, would find him in the end and so he resolved that perhaps The Retreat was a good place to start.

Then the story he had been searching for came to him. Amy Bentley, the wife of Mark Bentley of the law firm Harrison and Partners at Law, was on the same plane. The paper had been tracking the law firm under suspicion for money laundering. Liam was concerned that companies like that could continue to be dodgy, if there were fewer journalists around to follow through on the story. The law firm's representation for the Barretts and its win on rezoning a section of the harbour had hit the front pages. The public was mad but not fed up enough. There was too much complacency and not enough pressure on political will to change the zoning laws. He wondered what a woman like Amy Bentley was doing going to the same retreat as he was. It didn't go with her husband's party life but then Liam had never paid much attention to what her side of the story was in his investigations. She looked downtrodden, as though she'd lost something valuable. Liam wondered then what else Dusty was up to with the gathering he'd collected this Easter.

The other woman in the party was an Irish lady who intrigued Liam from the moment she got on the plane. The way her hands touched the window as the sun entered the cabin, reminded him of himself as a boy. She looked cold and she seemed to want to warm up with the thought of the sun outside, rather than the actual effect of it. There was a quietness to her too as if she had nothing left to say about life and he wondered what had brought her to the weekend. In profile, the light seemed to dance across her greying hair which still showed threads of a golden red. They got into conversation and introduced themselves. Then he helped Eileen down the passenger stairs and she held so tightly to him, it was as if she wasn't about to ever let him go.

'Can I ask ye a question? Just why are ye goin' to the retreat? Is it healin' y're after now?' He could feel her fragility. But there was a strength in her eyes which seemed to hold a childlike hope.

'I'm a friend of the caretaker. He thinks I might need time off.'

'Yer eyes are familiar. They've got a look about them I've seen somewhere before.'

'Piercing, I've been told. As if I'm looking further into something than I should be. I'm always being told that I'm a bit too thoughtful and I should just ease up a bit.' He tried to make the comment light-hearted to Eileen. He didn't want to speak openly just yet in front of Mrs Bentley who was behind them as they got into the retreat bus. Usually, he kept his eyes down. It was a shyness but also a defence against being accused of sniffing out a story.

'Yer name's Irish, y'know. Have you ever been home?' Eileen was being inquisitive and Liam knew how much the Irish liked to know connections.

'No, I've never been. My mother said my name means 'warrior' and 'protector'. She said she gave it to me to remind me of my destiny. I'm not sure what she meant. My parents passed away a few years ago.' It was his first moment of the retreat and he was opening up more than he had expected or wanted to. He was going to help Dusty out but surprisingly he was being drawn into something inside that felt like it was ready to come out as well.

That night at Liam's window in his cabin, the full moon captured him in its flood of light. It's when you forget yourself that others see you and in that moment he saw Amy Bentley come to her window and look out. He thought they both recognised that they were here for more than the obvious rest time. He wondered what it was like to live with a man like Mark Bentley. His reputation was smooth but deadly and Liam thought she either had that menace in her herself, or else she was a victim of his charisma. He felt sorry for a woman who came into the orbit of such corruption.

There was an unthreading as he sat at the small desk in the cabin, doodling away with the pencil and paper provided. The lines on the page were drawn sharp and he could feel how his hand gripped the pencil too tightly for an evening they were meant to relax in. Come to think of it, his body was too tight all over, now that he noticed. It was a state he was used to. He'd noted recently how he was waking at home with his body clenched even more, in almost a foetal position. Coincidence maybe but Dusty's call had come at the right time when he really needed to get away. Mrs Bentley's presence at the same retreat was even more of a coincidence though. Where this story could go was curious.

He'd been tracking her husband's social and work engagements trying to filter the everyday from the suspicious. In a city that felt like one big party, if you were rich enough to indulge, Mark Bentley had his fair share. Now the editor wanted Liam to report on his fun times, as if the press were mainly there to boost fame rather than decipher its menace or its camouflage for something more sinister. Not that there weren't many people content with the status quo. Liam questioned why he couldn't just join in though and make life easy for himself.

FAKE NEWS

For Liam, the tweet that had convinced him to accept Dusty's offer had come overnight: second rate reporting from a second rate journalist #fake news. The world had changed in its reporting. People got their news from spurious sources. It was easier that way. On air shock jocks were already taking calls from commuters stuck on the M4 or any other of the clogged roads they were on in peak hour traffic.

'Hey, isn't that Liam Patterson the same reporter who stirred things up so tax payers' money was wasted on that court case just recently? Haven't we got better things to spend our money on, honestly?'

'You sound irate, John. I hear you. Yes, fake news is everywhere these days. You just can't tell who to believe anymore.'

'Too right you can't. The money coming into this city is building the economy. We all know that. Without people investing in Sydney we'd all be out of a job.'

'That's what I've been saying, John. Now what would this idiot Patterson know about mining and what's good for the country when he can't even get the law straight about property rights. We have a solid citizen in the name of Barrett whom he mercilessly attacked just recently. Tried to make some connection with the banks and was laughed out of town. I mean can't you just see him typing away in some squirrel hole while the rest of us Aussies get on with it.'

'I'm with you there, Mate. No wonder no-one wants to read the news anymore.'

'That's why you need to tune into me, John. I'll make your day and keep the sunshine on your dial.' An upbeat jingle then played to complete the message as it segued into an ad.

Liam had been called into the office. His editor was frank, even a little hostile. The social file was handed to him to cover instead of his usual investigative reporting. They were giving him a break. 'Oh and look, Liam. We've had a call from Harrison and Partners. They're the legal firm…'

'I know who they are. Was it signed Mark Bentley?'

'You don't know what it said first.'

'I can guess. Libel? Slander? Some misquoting or taking something out of context? They attack through the courts. It's an old game.'

'Yes, well one we can't afford anymore. You're going to have to lay off reporting on the property and bank conspiracy you think is happening out there somewhere.'

'It's not somewhere. It can be traced to the Barretts and the deals they seem magically to engineer.'

'Look, you haven't got enough evidence and no-one will back you in court or else their heads are on the block.'

'Well, the only conspiracy I can see here is the conspiracy of silence.'

He remembered watching Mark Bentley dining with John Barrett in an exclusive restaurant by the harbour. A feast of hubris. They must have thought the city was their own but Liam had seen punters fall before this. Perception was everything. If only truth wasn't so elusive. Liam had constructed evidence of suspected money laundering through the banks but it was insufficient to go to print. Then the hate-mail intensified. A new age bullying that was effective in a world where appearances shifted with doubt.

The call from Dusty cut through precisely because it was so innocent. Liam could hear the anguish he was feeling when outside forces were set to take advantage of a world he held a promise to. The promise for Liam was in the reverse. The office up-date had replaced the chipped melamine desk and 70's swirling orange wallpaper. This new investment in the newsroom was technology minus the worth of journalists, with sackings expected. After all, it was convenient for some to keep the public ignorant. The sleek black metal lamp hung over his workspace. Its arm bended precariously above his head, throwing a spotlight on the computer screen which held a mirrored image of his own worn out face staring back. There was now or never to decide. Dusty was urging the visit for Easter, a few days away. Would he come?

He'd said yes, packed his desk and walked out with the conviction he'd be back in a few days after a shot of green forest and blue air to settle the agitation he couldn't easily shake. What could the country offer that he couldn't find in a dip at the beach or a run in the park? It was just that he wasn't really doing these things anymore. They were still active in his imagination though, to make him believe he still could.

SAD MUSIC

The first morning of their musical challenge from Sergio, Liam saw Eileen on the path ahead and thought she might like to stroll together for a while. He liked the way she held her shoulders upright. You could see she'd had a hard life by the way she moved with effort but at the same time there was a determination in the way she picked up objects and studied their form. When he reached her, her hands were full of seeds. She said she had tried to make sense of the sound coming from some of the hollow ones.

'All I can make out of it I'm afraid, is sad music, Liam. I don't want to go disturbin' ye now.'

'Not at all, Eileen. I think the point is to let nature bring out what's there inside. I guess this retreat is a safe place to try.' He felt like putting his arm through hers but hesitated. He didn't want her to think he was too familiar when they'd only just met. But he couldn't help but be drawn into something about her gentle presence.

'It's grand, David … Aw dear.' She put her hand to her mouth as if the name she had spoken held a meaning she couldn't resist to try.

Liam looked at her sideways and she apologised that she'd made a mistake and was just thinking about someone else and another name came out. She looked at him as if the sight of someone else was fading from her eyes and there was only Liam left standing in the spot. 'I get a feeling this place has ghosts. Hopefully they're friendly ones.' He tried to be funny but she caught him in her stare. Whatever she was seeing was a mystery to him. He left her on the path to the hill and made his way into a section of the rainforest which led down to the river. He felt Eileen was standing watching him go and he sensed a longing in her that he guessed the idea of finding the music could bring out.

The forest was still and dark early in the morning and so dense it felt like he was breathing in its clammy breath. He stopped and sat on a rock beside the path, deciding to listen as instructed. He hadn't really noticed before how alive the place really was. There were bird noises surrounding him, shifting focus as they called to each other. He could hear the whip bird with its high note and cracking reply and he knew that there were really two birds, male and female, in the conversation. Then the cat bird started like a baby's cry and he felt a loss inside that brought tears. The loss of both parents together was a shock he hadn't been able to overcome.

The house, still filled with their things, meant nothing with them gone. The days at the paper were becoming ferocious. People were losing faith in the paper's mission and each other. He was coming into middle age alone. He hadn't established a relationship that endured. He had no clues as to where he fitted in. In reality he felt like crying like that catbird, a pathetic wail that the voices around seemed to be emulating. It seemed like the forest was feeding him back what was inside. His frustration. His loss. It felt like the forest was becoming part of who he was or was he becoming part of it? Beth had said, 'Just let go and be easy,' and so he found myself in a daydream where the vines and the leaves grew around him and in him. A living thing that the birds knew to call to and he knew to answer back.

He didn't know how long he sat there but when he opened his eyes and refocused, Liam felt calm. Something had shifted and he could feel layers of loss had emptied to nothing. His breath was steady and he had a reassuring feeling that work would sort itself out. How to live alone was another thing. He realised that his parents had framed many of his artworks that were on the walls of the house they had left to him. He didn't quite know why he doubted himself so much, when they had believed in him. Maybe it was time to give painting more effort. Dusty had spoken about a cabin or shack in the woods where there was someone special who he thought Liam would like to meet. Dusty was taking care of him for some reason and Liam thought that Dusty must think he had some powers of persuasion if it was Liam he'd picked to join in the fight. 'Just paint what you see and show it to the people in the city.' Dusty had said that a painting and a story, done by the right person, could bring the land to life in people's hearts. Liam wasn't sure how he was the right one but Dusty had said he'd seen Liam's work on his website and it was exactly what he was after.

Liam was calm then and sketched what he could see of the valley from a clearing in the forest. Below, the river wound through like a living thing. He knew there were changes happening where rivers were being given the status of a person in law. It had happened in New Zealand and India and so he started to draw the river as a woman with curves and flowing hair making up the tributaries. Bends cut down through the farmland and a lonely timber cottage, he saw, lay growing amongst the weeds to be painted in. He wondered who had abandoned the house so long ago. A crumbling building sat beside it and it seemed to be the burnt-out remains of something. He thought about how dreams die along with the seasons and wondered how new dreams might have the possibility of growing amongst the weeds that spring up.

He could hear his mother saying, 'One day, Liam, you'll know who you are meant to be. Know where you truly belong.' It wasn't easy to start again after the accident which left him alone. His mother had encouraged his creativity and study to become a journalist but had also said to not to look too far into things, that some things were better left unsaid. He wondered what the silent gaps were in the unspoken words she could no longer convey. Gaps that grew weeds in the spaces of his memory, like the cottage in the distance. His father too was a silent figure. He had the belief that a child could only learn when they were ready to receive. It had the effect on Liam that all he could think to do was discover and that fuelled his curiosity to research when something didn't feel right, when a story needed to be told.

The story of Amy Bentley was intriguing. He'd seen her in the social pages at times but not for a while now. Surely you couldn't live with someone and not be suspicious of their affairs. But then maybe Mark Bentley was a good actor. He'd acted on behalf of the Barretts and now the mining company and although it couldn't be proved he'd acted outside the law, he worked within the unethical grey zones where legislation hadn't quite caught up on all the nuances of opportunistic peoples' actions. Who better to be one step ahead of the law than a lawyer himself?

Through the clearing Liam could see Amy Bentley by the river and he added her female shape to the foreground. The elegant line he drew didn't quite fit with the thought she might be tied into her husband's possible criminal activities. The way she picked up objects and discarded them whimsically, had a casual innocence. A woman with more sinister intent had a certainty of movement, a consciousness of game playing, a catlike poise held within striking distance. Amy Bentley had none of these qualities. Whatever her reason for being here, she appeared to be looking for answers like he was.

Her decision to go swimming that night, he thought, was a dangerous idea. He found he needed to check she was safe and so he had made his way to the river and saw her as she crossed to the rock on the far side. As she pulled herself out of the water, he saw her naked body was gleaming in the moonlight and he thought she looked serene in the stillness of it all. But then he heard her crying and calling out to someone he couldn't make out. He knew she'd think he was perving when all he could see was line and form and an extension of the river which wound into the shape of a woman that seemed to float amongst the trees and disappear from view. The Retreat was turning into a place of discovery and Liam wondered if in time everything would be explained.

THE PROMISE

Dusty's first sighting of the valley was from a trek that skirted the ranges along the eastern seaboard. His dad had said he'd know the valley by the wide delta that splayed out before it. Not many valleys had such width and diversity. Mostly, a river would split into a few arms before entering the sea, but this valley had many islands dotted across it with pasture and dairy farms spread out across the flood plains. He saw it from a height as he traversed from valley to valley along the ridge line that formed a barrier to the western slopes and deserts beyond. To the east lay most of Australia's population in its fertile belt. The valley, his father had said, held a promise for him to keep and like Abraham he was sending his son Dusty, to a promised land.

The reality though was far from the biblical renaissance he had imagined. When he reached the property he was sent to find, instead of the saw-mill and farmhouse, the place was left to rot. Vines were overtaking the veranda of the timber house and Dusty guessed the memories contained inside were boarded in as well. The saw-mill looked like a fire had destroyed the working parts of it. The metal roof had fallen in on the saw which was rusted and charred. Something had gone seriously wrong, something his father had not told him about when he'd spoken of the journey he said that he needed Dusty to take. He wanted him to find Old Jack and see if he was still alive. Dusty set up his tent by a water hole at a bend of the river further up from the carnage and set about making camp. Whatever had happened, he felt the need to stay and survey the area for clues.

Under the water, flitches from the mill lay like dead men below the surface. He wondered how someone, his dad had admired and spoken about so much when Dusty was growing up, could use the waterhole as a dumping ground for off-cuts. His dad had said he owed it to Old Jack to help him finish his dream. He'd convinced

Dusty to come here to discover something of his dad's past and Dusty's future, he'd said. They'd been exchanging letters until a few years back and Dusty saw with each letter, his dad's dark behaviour from his Vietnam War legacy, had softened. Dusty was curious about what it was that his dad thought he could learn from Jack.

Further up the slope, beyond the rock that jutted out on the other side, was evidence of replanting of the forests. Regrowth was strong into places where loggers, like his dad, had once cut. Stands of mountain ash reached up to the high ridge and Dusty wondered if it was Jack who had made such an effort to rehabilitate a land that he had once felled so harshly.

Fresh tracks of a dog, or dingo perhaps, led through the bush and up into stands of rainforest. Dusty wondered if anyone was left living up there and what concern they might have if they thought he was trespassing on their property. He couldn't wait for the morning though having come this far and so with a miner's torch strapped to his forehead, he followed the path that led into the bush. The track was well defined and he could see beside the dog paws, a human set of footprints as well. The size of the impression meant he was a big man, just like his dad had described him. It hadn't long been raining and the muddy imprints indicated that someone had been here only a short while before. He wondered that if it was Jack, had he seen Dusty come onto the property and set up camp?

Dusty had come across from the Wild Rivers National Park with only a back pack and a tent. He wasn't too concerned about being in the bush at night. He'd grown used to the night birds signalling danger but he could never figure out whose side they were on. His dad had taught him well. His time in the jungles of Vietnam had heightened his senses and the knowledge had been passed on from father to son. 'Take care with each step and keep your focus. You're part of nature but that includes the dark side.' He wasn't sure what he was heading towards but something about the stillness of the night, helped him to remain calm.

Fireflies were out, dancing in a grove overhung by a rocky ledge. Luminous fungi also lit the way and once or twice he spotted the still red eyes of mammals hiding behind tree stumps and fallen branches. Although the track wasn't wide there had been care in its construction with little damage done to the vegetation on either side.

Through the layers of night, a light glowed within the forest up ahead. Dusty sensed maybe a clearing was nearby but if it was, it would have disturbed little of the landscape in which it sat. When he came across a small timber bridge, an octagonal hut sat beyond, with light streaming like a lantern from its glass cupola. A kelpie dog lying on the front step to the veranda seemed to be awaiting his arrival. There was no mad barking but a softened yelp that had the old man inside come out and stand in the open door frame, with hands on hips grinning.

'I see you've arrived. What took you so long?'

The man's boots rested on the edge of the doorstep and he stepped out to greet Dusty in woollen socks, overalls and a sheep skin coat that made him look like part man, part animal. His eyes though still belonged to a child. There was something in the vitality of the welcome that alerted Dusty to the energy he was entering into. He started to question whether he was up for the challenge. Inside the cottage, the walls were covered in book shelves. Stacks of papers lined the desk which sat beside the fire. Although Jack had candlelight for mood, Dusty also observed a series of solar panels that sat beside the hut for electricity. Here was an enigma. Instead of a wild old man Dusty had envisaged from the devastation of the buildings at the front of the property, standing before him was a man who showed he was at peace with his surroundings and was able to live comfortably with little.

'I'm looking for Jack Turner. My father, Glen Boland, said I might find him here and I'd be made welcome.' Dusty could tell though the old man had already recognised him.

'Glen's contacted me since you set out on your trek. I hadn't been able to answer his letters before now but with you on your way I had some hope things might change a bit. Answer to my prayers.' The old man twisted a set of prayer beads wrapped around his wrist. 'I was getting worried you might have got lost. The National Trail you were on can be tricky in parts. You must be some bushman alright, just like your dad.'

Dusty stood watching him. His hair was greying but still full, with flecks of the dark curly hair he once had, keeping him youthful. His was a heavy brow-line but the eyes underneath were soft and blue, fading at the edges to grey as they aged. Dusty's dad hadn't seen Jack since his dad was a young man himself and Dusty wondered if his dad would recognise now the old man he had sent him to see.

'You might as well come into the shack and I'll tell you my story and hopefully your place in it.'

Dusty hesitated at the doorway not sure of his place here and whether or not he really wanted what was expected of him from an age that was long past. The old man continued on but seemed to sense the indecision to commit to someone else's dream. He called over his shoulder to give Dusty the space to decide for himself. 'What's stopping you, Son?' They were the words Dusty had heard his dad use again and again when he had hesitated to move forward with his life. It was in that moment he realised the impact Old Jack had had on his dad and what influence his dad had sent Dusty to.

'Nothing, Mr Turner. Nothing's stopping me at all.' The leap across the gap of restraint released a tension in Dusty he didn't expect. As if the river was carrying him swiftly now, the night became a set of discoveries of how Dusty's father had known Jack's son when they had both worked in the saw-mill. 'Keeping your dad and my son working when the surf was big on the coast down there was an effort but they'd always work twice as hard when they came back.' Jack laughed at the memory but then a redness came into his cheeks and he stared into a past Dusty couldn't fathom but could see its effect in the silence. Dusty thought about how his dad had said he was being sent as a way to help heal the wounds of the past. Jack had plans to rebuild the property from a place where trees were once logged, to a place that people could come to for rejuvenation. Dusty was relatively young and strong and just the sort of help Jack would need to realise his plans of constructing a garden retreat, beyond the burnt out remains of the saw-mill. Not that Dusty's dad had realised how bad things had become for Jack but in his silence over the last few years, Dusty thought that his dad must have guessed.

'I saw you looking at the flitches under the water.' Dusty recognised that Old Jack was a step ahead at every move. It seemed Jack had been watching and waiting not only for Dusty's arrival but for his character to be revealed as well. 'It's something I'm trying to recover, you'll see. Here, take a look at what each piece of timber I'm salvaging represents.'

One by one Jack took out a refined piece of worked timber. 'I like to sand what's in there. It's just like life, if you let it. I sell the pieces in the local market and that helps me buy things for my project.'

Jack was holding a smooth piece of rounded timber shaped like an egg. He kept rubbing his gnarled hands across it, as if it was in some form of incubation. In the candlelight the warm honey colour glowed. 'This is my favourite piece. You can whittle things away too far you know; its knowing when to stop. I like the way this piece fits into my hand. It feels like it's part of me now, just like this place. Here, I want to show you my plans for the retreat.'

By the fire that night, with the kelpie, called Joe, at his feet, Jack sketched the shape of the main building and huts situated on the bank where Dusty had set up camp earlier. 'It's round, you see, to keep the energy contained but flowing. You can't hide in corners in a round house but you can join in the flow of movement that builds up in a natural way. All tribes gather in circles to meet and I want this place to recreate an ancient ritual site for healing.'

In spite of his calm acceptance, Dusty sensed an urgency in Jack as if he had an awareness that he was running out of time. 'I thought you were my prodigal son returning but I know that will never happen.' He looked distracted and turned to the fire with his back to Dusty. 'That's why Glen had said you would be capable of stepping up if I were to show you the reason why you were sent here.'

There was a hesitancy now as if the request he was making was held in a balance of forces beyond his control. Outside, an owl sat on the veranda post, solitary and still, before lifting its wings silently into the darkness. Dusty wondered whether Jack had been feeding it and whether it was a regular visitor to the cabin. He sensed it delivering a message to its surroundings that Glen's son had arrived and Jack's plan now was in motion.

As he returned to his camp that evening, Dusty turned off the head lamp and made his way down the path with his eyes adjusting to the darkness. The stream nearby followed in a swollen rushing after the rain and as he entered the campsite, he could see how the waterhole was filling and spilling over the rapids to fall in a torrent further downstream.

He'd placed his tent on a rise where the waters weren't reaching, beyond the blackened mill and the empty house and the story there that was left to unfold. He thought, 'This is where we'll begin tomorrow.' He'd decided from Jack's story that this was where he'd settle until the job was complete.

CONFLICTING VOICES

The build began with the putting up of Dusty's hut first. Jack had begun to assemble the main frames and Dusty had enough building experience from learning what he could from his father back home, to create the first shingle roofed cabin.

It hadn't been easy settling into the rhythms of Jack, with his early morning starts and relentless purpose, which came to Dusty in fragments. Dusty could sense Jack's urgency. He hoped to discover more of the story he had committed to but knew enough of Jack now to wait for the right time for it to be revealed. So, he settled into what was to become his home for the next few years.

Jack was busy building the garden and communicating with the neighbours about self-sufficiency and bartering anything that was excess. Each week the local market in the valley held stores of locally produced organic foods, crafts and artworks like Jack's sculptures. He had quite a name for himself, with city people driving out to buy one of Jack Turner's figures for their luxury apartments in town.

'You're not charging enough for them, Jack. They're taking advantage of you, I think.' Dusty knew a particular curator had arrived and bought a number of pieces at bargain prices to sell in his gallery.

'It's not the money I'm interested in, Dusty. What I'm selling is a dream of the value of nature. I want people to understand that when they feel the timber in their fingers that it is a living thing worth protecting, just like themselves. I want this retreat we're building to signal that it is important to pay attention to life and not squander it.' Dusty could feel Jack's intention to get his message out no matter what. At night Jack would be up till late going over and over the direction he was taking. The stacks of notes and papers in his cabin continued to build as he researched the best methods to help people cope with a life Jack saw as complicated.

'It's getting crazier out there and there's not too much guidance you can rely on. There are so many conflicting voices.' Jack went on to explain how he had learnt to come back after tragedy and how the forest had been his saviour in the end. 'I learnt to accept and just be still. Just being here as part of the place brought out an inner strength I didn't realise I had.' Jack spoke about learning to be gentle with himself instead of letting the anger destroy him. 'I shifted my thinking little by little. I just wish I'd known more about letting go while Mary was still alive. She bore me well with her patience, you know.' He went on to tell Dusty that in the end though, she couldn't bear the loss of her son to a senseless war.

In the evening by Jack's fire, the two of them would unravel the past that had brought them together. 'You may not have known that your father and my son were in Vietnam together.' It had taken a long time for Jack to broach this subject and Dusty wondered whether Jack had waited until he could trust him. His father had rarely spoken about the war. After returning home, he said he was treated like an outcast. No-one knew what to do with the Vietnam vets. There'd been so much protest and arguments about conscription. Other returned soldiers didn't seem to understand the kind of war they'd been through. Although it was on the TV sets and people could watch the fighting, there was an unreality to it that followed the soldiers back to Australia. No myths had been built up and no-one wanted to see a war return that had ended in defeat. His dad spoke of Nashos returned without rehabilitation, his voice dying to a whisper when he recalled their active service to a life on the farm, in a breath and a war between.

'Dad just held it in. Sometimes I'd think he would burst with it.' Dusty was caught in the memory of his father's tense silence. The pacing on the veranda in the red sky of evening. 'The fire on the horizon,' he called it. And then the whisky bottle would be emptied and his mother would wait till he fell asleep on the lounge or until the demons came out. He never took it out on her or Dusty physically. But what was there to do with a husband and a father who held the poisoned cup to his lips? A man who still lived in the jungle with the eyes of his dead mate open to the sky.

'They were in the same lottery. David never returned but your dad did.' Jack was being careful. He didn't know how much Glen Boland had disclosed about the battle that David was killed in. He'd counselled Glen for years through letters they'd exchanged. Jack had to accept a dead son and Glen had to accept there was nothing he could do to bring his mate back.

Dusty held Jack's eyes. He could see his mother holding his father in her arms, rocking him like a baby. Telling him he'd be alright. 'I never knew Dad's mate, David, was your son. I'm sorry.'

'Best mates and you look just like him too.' He was trying to be light-hearted but Jack was looking into the past. The send-off where Mary cried the moment he went down the drive. How she'd kept her back straight though while he'd gone through the door. And then the agony and the gulping of the tears as he drove away. If he'd looked back he would have seen her on her knees. But David never knew the impact. He was too young to understand a mother is tied to a son forever.

'Dad never told me anything about the connection. He spoke about you separately as if he couldn't bring himself to speak about the horrors he had witnessed.' He looked at Jack as if the words he had to say were words his father had entrusted him with, words to come out when the time was right. 'All I know was that Dad said that his mate had his back in battle and it was his mate, David, who took the bullet and not him.'

Dusty watched as Jack sat still and looked into the fire as if in some memory from long ago. 'Did he say anything else? Anything at all. Mary and I were never given the full story you see, just a dead son who was never returned to us.'

Dusty held back. He had more to say but whether this was the moment he wasn't sure. He'd brought the story together so far and which way to proceed was up to more than he could predict. 'Just that he loved you both. Dad said he spoke of you a lot.'

'It killed his mother you know; she never got over it.' Jack then stood still by the fire with the hammer limply in his hand. It was the first time Dusty had seen him lose that certainty he had that his project was what meant the most to him. This was what Dusty had waited for: the unfolding of Jack in all his painful memory. Dusty stilled to witness the motivation for his building of the retreat, the replanting of the forest and the desire to bring people to a place for healing. Another fragment had escaped.

Putting the hammer down, Jack pulled from his pocket the timber egg he always kept close to him. He held it tenderly like a rock that had protected him. 'I did this for Mary. The whole idea was for Mary to be safe, but she didn't make it through. I've failed mostly but this place is where David was born and Mary died, so I'm going to make it mean something while I've still got breath.'

'What happened to the sawmill, Jack? Did a fire go through?'

Jack stood still as if the memory of that night was beyond words. He bowed his head and then shifted slightly, digging his hands into the hearth to regain a strength to begin. 'I burnt it down myself the night Mary died. After that I never went back inside the home. Too many memories.' He waited while the past played out before him until some resolve was reached. 'So, I built a place in the woods instead of going crazy and set about planting trees instead of cutting them. It was the only way I knew how to survive when I had nothing left.' He held still then as if the time was becoming right. 'I want you to come up to the shack later tonight, I have something I need to show you.'

'What about the home, Jack? I can fix it up if you are ready.' Dusty had already thought about how he might repaint the blistered timbers and redo the broken veranda of the old homestead but it took permission to enter into another's sorrow and Dusty knew that only Jack could say when that was to be.

'Not yet, Son. Time will settle. In time.' He looked towards Dusty as if together he might walk through the front door with the silver knocker and enter the kitchen where Mary baked her bread. He might step into the bedroom where they had made their love into a great and sorrowful thing. Above the bed, the Jesus image with the bleeding heart would carry their names engraved. He might wait at the door to the room which held David's things, with the box under the bed the only thing salvaged to keep. But one step at a time was all he had to walk right now. The opening of vine covered memories would be a delicate thing to hold.

'Come back at night. Some things are best seen in the dark.

GHOST GUM

That evening as Dusty entered the cabin, Jack was waiting for him with a determined look in his eyes that said this was the time to reveal himself. The fire was lit and Jack had two chairs placed beside it and a small table with an album on it. He uncorked a red wine from the vineyard he had planted on the site. The drink was rough but warm on the back of his tongue. Jack held onto the album and slowly opened it to reveal a picture of the family that was his when he was only in his early twenties. Mary was holding the baby David and smiling, Madonna like.

'She's beautiful, Jack. No wonder you were in love.'

'The only love of my life. I didn't need anyone else. When she said, 'I do,' I knew I was the luckiest man on earth.'

'You only had the one child?'

'It was a rough birth.' He hesitated at the memory of Mary in emergency and the decision he'd always held onto as the right one. 'We almost lost her and I said, 'Enough.' I couldn't take the chance. David was all we needed anyway.'

'You were lucky, Jack.'

'Till my luck ran out.' He paused again and this time the story was ripe to come out. 'We nearly lost him before, you know.'

'David, you mean?'

'It's been hard to forgive myself for not being enough but it was all I could do.' Jack was talking as if Dusty knew about the history and kept breaking into snippets of a story of a lost boy.

'Are you saying that David was lost as a boy, Jack?'

'In the bush up the back here. Overnight when he was three.' Jack was recalling the terror of the discovery when he'd turned to bring his little boy back down from the mill to the homestead below. It had only taken a short moment of distraction when David had followed the butterfly instead of the path he'd been sent on. Jack had turned back for a moment to collect a tool and when he'd turned around David was gone.

'The whole valley was called up. There were hundreds you know searching through the bush.' Jack recalled the desperate calling that went on through the night.

'And what about Mary, Jack?'

'She was away on the coast with her family. I'd been entrusted. It was the first time she'd let me, you see. I don't know what I would have done if she'd been here.'

'What happened, Jack?'

'A moment I'll never forget when George Fischer found him lying under a tree the next morning and called out to come. He was alive and hungry.' Jack stalled then and the memory held him into a place of silence that Dusty didn't feel he had the right to open again. He thought in time more might be revealed but for now the threads of David's life were becoming a stronger weave to him.

What Dusty had now to tell Jack was a possibility only. A needle in a giant haystack that he didn't know if he had the right to say. The potential to cause more pain was real. He'd been holding onto the promise that the story to be delivered to Jack would come at the right time. Dusty recalled his father saying, 'Just see if you think Jack is up to it. If not, keep it to yourself. Not everything can be righted in the end.' But Dusty had seen how Jack had faced his demons and survived.

'Um, Jack. You did ask me if there was anything else Dad had said about David.'

Jack braced himself. He'd waited years for anything that might add to the knowledge of David that he could hold onto. 'Go on. What have you got to say, Son?'

'Well, Dad did tell me of some things that were said before the battle. Dad said that David had spoken of his parents, about how they didn't want him to go and how he was sorry for the harm it might cause them.' He watched while Jack took in the words of concern that David had expressed. So he did understand after all. It was his duty then that he went for. A blind faith in honour.

'And then he spoke of someone else.' Jack's eyes looked straight into Dusty as if there was some hope that a connection to David still existed. That through that connection a part of David could be brought back to life. 'He mentioned a woman he had met and had left back in Sydney. Dad said he was going home to Eileen and was intending to bring her up to meet his parents as soon as he could. Dad said he had fallen in love with Eileen and he was intending to marry her.'

At that moment Dusty saw Jack as an old tree that had been shaken so hard it looked like it could crack and fall but instead he rallied. 'I want you to find Eileen. If she's still alive, I want to meet her for myself.' He was resolute. There was an urgent pleading in him that Dusty couldn't resist and he resolved that he would need to find Eileen. He only hoped that she had stayed in Australia and not returned to Ireland where she came from. Dusty wondered how this man had withstood the assaults of life, locked in a battle with fate. How had Jack come to a place of peace and now a new hope that out there life had a new beginning for him?

'There's something else I need to show you now and the night is the best time to see it. Come with me, Son.' Jack grabbed the torch from the table and set up out the back of the shack, along a path that wound through the darkness of the forest. He knew the path well but Dusty found himself stumbling over roots along the path trying to keep up with him. He didn't explain anything but that was usual for Jack. He didn't feel the need to mostly. He wouldn't be showing Dusty if it wasn't worthwhile.

Dusty saw the white gum, like a ghost, rise up out of the track. 'You can see the scars from all its battles with bushfires and disease but it's still standing from way before white man arrived.' Jack sent the light into the top branches and a sugar glider leapt off and out, into a leap of faith into the darkness. 'They've adapted to glide like a parachute from predators. There's a family up there and I have learnt that if we destroy their habitat they will be endangered. You see, this is the tree where they found David with grass stains around his mouth.' He quietly revealed to Dusty that it was this tree that he'd come to when Mary died. He said he had sat here until he could move again. 'I couldn't cut this one down and now this is the tree that has saved me.'

Then Jack looked at Dusty hopefully. 'You'll find Eileen, won't you, Son. You'll bring Eileen home to me now.'

'I'll do my best, Jack.'

'There's one more thing I need you to see. It's been a battle but I feel now is the time to face a new threat I didn't feel I had the strength for.' Back at the cabin, Jack pressed an official letter into Dusty's hands. He recognised straight away that it was from a law firm in the city. It read that there was the intention to secure access for mining exploration in the area. It seemed to assume that the farmers would be open to negotiation and if not, the company would be seeking arbitration for their rights. 'They've got no respect for anything but their own greedy ends. Can you imagine the people here trying to farm, with mining along the valley? It will destroy us and I'm not going to let that happen.' Jack looked like he was seeing the ghost gum being felled. The only tie that he had left being taken from him in a scrounging for profit.

Dusty looked at the letter, with legal jargon highlighting rights to mine. Inside were the dreams of others who did not know the valley but could sniff its wealth. What lay under the ground was where their glory lay without regard for what was living above. Dusty pictured wild habitats dispossessed in the battle that was one sided. Jack had realised where we humans sat amongst the inhabitants: on top. But he also realised that that came with responsibility, for now and for the future as well.

He'd seen other farmers destroyed as mining had come to their valley. A family would hold out while all the farms around would let go, the man like a hunted animal himself with the wild eyes of being cornered, trapping his children as well. He knew Jack would be one of those men who was determined to stay. They'd be carrying him out in a box. Dusty knew that for sure.

'It's OK, Jack. We'll see what we can do. If we tell the people out there our story, there's a chance we'll be heard and common sense will prevail.' Dusty had determined he could stand the fight his father had sent him to. He wondered though if it was a simple equation of David and Goliath. Like David they had a true sense of destiny in their hands but Dusty wasn't sure if myths existed to be broken.

'And when people come to the retreat they'll see that they are part of the story too.'

'Yes, Jack. We're all part of this story. It just takes time for us to listen.'

IF YOU BELIEVE

Dusty had said he'd show Amy the platypus. Dusk was the best time, he'd said. As Amy made her way to the waterhole, her body continued to open to the possibilities. An unspoken language had started to rise to the surface. With Mark she had sunk her desires a long time before the end. What he couldn't see in her, she started to believe didn't exist at all. She saw how Mark would chase after a new thing until he was satisfied and then discard it just as quickly. The friends had felt the neglect when he became too busy to call. Too urgent to prioritise love. She could see it was a delicate thing that didn't announce itself too readily, just a softly spoken promise that she hoped would return to her again one day.

That morning, Dusty had spoken of the need to protect the land and the wild habitats. Amy felt he was pressing her to see the urgency and she let him know that she was concerned with the way the city was changing as well. 'Unrestrained Utopia,' she called it and Dusty said it sounded like an oxymoron. He wanted to know about green buildings being built and they discussed how architects who were trying to bring a balance back into people's lives, were fighting for a place. A Tower of Babel was being forged in the confusion of voices, he'd said and he spoke again of the simple need for nature to be present and respected.

She told him about how the invitation to spend Easter at the retreat meant more to her than he realised it could. Amy wanted him to know that the confusion in her mind was about how she dealt with relationships. She was concerned about the environment but being a city girl it wasn't her main focus until now. She told him about how she couldn't read people's intentions and how she'd been taken advantage of on a number of occasions, her desire to please outweighing her intuition. He had looked embarrassed and turned away and Amy wanted to reassure him that she enjoyed his company no matter what.

She saw him then on the bank as she arrived for their meeting. The water mirrored the sunset of golds and crimson and the surface of the water flowed softly. She could see the ripples on the surface but as she approached the bank they disappeared. He was waiting in a way that looked distracted as he rolled a stone at his foot down the bank. It sunk heavily and Amy could see how his shoulders sunk with it as if he had a weight of his own to carry. She approached softly. She thought that maybe he was just like that wild creature she'd come here to see. How to be present to him was foreign to her, just as being present to herself had been until now. 'I'm sorry did I frighten them?'

He turned to her with a confused look, then rearranged himself and gestured for her to sit. 'Don't worry. Just sit quietly and they will surface. You just have to be patient.' She thought the patience he meant was more than waiting for the platypus. She'd seen a struggle in him in his urgency to build the retreat, but for her it was like sitting in her comfort zone for the first time in a long time. The sign above the fireplace on the first night, 'Simply Me', began to make sense. The time with Mark when he behaved so cruelly towards her, was mostly the battle he had within himself. He couldn't be kind when he'd lost any sense of who he really was. Now the presence of Dusty seemed real enough for her to want to be there, a quiet place where real conversation could start.

Then the creature surfaced and swam across the waterhole with its duck beak lying flat on the surface. She watched how it dived and stayed under and rose again to swim along. And then how a whole group of this strange animal who'd come out of their burrows, went about their business of foraging for food. She turned to Dusty but his look made her cautious. She'd seen that look before.

'They have venom you know. The male spur can be painful if you are pricked.' She could see he was warning her, calling on her to reconsider her motivation in the light of his own.

'I'm not sure what you mean, Dusty. Is there something you

need to tell me?'

He hesitated then. It was manipulative and he knew it. How she would take what he had to say was unknown and it was difficult to begin, 'I owe you an apology.'

'For what?' Mark had never apologised. He'd attacked in his style. She could see Dusty was upset with himself, upset for her.

'I'm sorry, Amy, but I didn't think everything through. I didn't understand that human beings need protecting as much as the environment.'

And then the story unfolded that he had sought Amy out because she was the wife of Mark Bentley, the lawyer who represented the mining company. He had heard they had split up and maybe Amy was willing to help him if she were to recognise the value of the retreat by being a participant here. He looked shattered that he had taken advantage of her and he said that he had realised that he was no different to the people she had told him about, who had taken advantage of her before.

Amy thought of the intrusion into her life now that appeared clinical. A darker deceit perhaps, which a veil of innocence had covered. At least Mark was obvious in his intent to win. She felt sick that for a moment she'd held onto a hope that wasn't real. 'So, did I get it wrong this morning? You seemed interested in getting to know me for myself. Am I wrong to think that?' The certainty of an answer that included her was suspended between. She wasn't sure she could take another defeat but then life was about getting up no matter what and Amy had been well schooled in that reality.

'I just felt the urgency to help Jack and the valley that's all. It was wrong to single you out. I know that. I was naïve.'

'Like me,' she thought.

He'd tried to help Jack by using her and yet their time on the ridge in the morning had opened up more than either of them understood. 'I can't expect anything from someone I'll only see for a few days and then they'll be gone back to the city. I can't hope you'll forgive me either.'

She was surprised. He'd asked the similar question about distance and time and relationship that she had. It meant that he'd been thinking about her like she'd been thinking about him. Yes, she could forgive him when she saw his honest intent now and so she braved the next question. 'So, Beth is your partner perhaps?' She was pushing his response. If she did have a short time, then she had decided that this chance to get to know a man she was beginning to dream about could not be missed. She needed to know what she was driving herself into. This time with her eyes open. They were facing each other honestly, trying to navigate the reasons why they'd both come to the river to meet.

'No, Beth and Sergio live in a property further down the valley. I've been helping Jack out for so long now I really haven't thought too much about relationships. It doesn't mean I don't want to though, with the right person.' His eyes were down and Amy could feel a tension that lay between the both of them. There was a restlessness Amy had seen on that first day, the way he swam with an urgent stroke. Something was struggling amongst the seeming calm of the place. Some outside forces held even the people who lived here to a wariness of purpose. Who to trust? What life was going to face you with? For all the desire to be at peace, the reality of life was volatile and changing. When it came to really communicating, it wasn't easy to let the layers of truth surface, in case the vulnerability was exposed and it was too fragile to survive.

Yet somehow Amy understood that there would always be another time when she wouldn't see others and their intentions so clearly. Instead what was happening, was that for the first time she was seeing herself clearly and what she really wanted. 'It's OK, Dusty. I'll help if I can but I don't think there's much I can do. We're not married now and I'm on my own.' She thought of the Mark she knew, celebrating the next win over people with less power. The way things worked, relied on who could afford to pay for that power and Mark and his firm were on the winning side with all its benefits.

'I thought maybe you could talk to him. Help him to understand that there's a value here that he's missing.' He looked fragile and scared the way he held his body into himself. It was not the sure swimmer she'd seen on the first morning. The man beside her was carrying a weight she knew too much about already, the weight of a battle he was preparing himself for, alone. 'I'm afraid it will kill Jack if the mines arrive.' And then he told Amy about how he'd been sent to help Jack build his dream.

'When my father came back from the war, he was beaten. It was the letters that Jack continued to send, that kept Dad going. Mum would wait for the post to arrive and every week they came until a few years ago. It was like Dad was his son. Dad was absent to me and Mum copped the anger in him as neglect. The letters shifted him slowly. I asked him what was changing in him and all he could answer was that he was learning to heal his guilt. Jack had told him the only person he needed to forgive was himself. I never understood the extent of that until I met Jack.'

They sat together past dusk until the chill settled in and it was time for the evening session. Amy could hear the machinery of the mines scraping up the valley, gouging out the waterways. She could see the birds, the black cockatoos screeching across the landscape in warning. The letters from the law firm would placate with the offerings of a payment or offer to buy and then one by one the smaller holdings further down the valley would pack up and give in. They'd be picked off one by one. That was the way Mark had said worked best. 'Piecemeal attack,' he called it. Ruthless none the less.

'I know a Barry Delany who might be of interest. I'll give him a call if you like.'

He turned to her then and the next moment his arm was around her and he was drawing her into the warmth of his body. It was sudden, unexpected and she didn't move from it at all. There was a quiet comfort in the way they both stared across the water, together in the same direction. She twisted the band on her finger and Dusty reached out to examine the sculpted gold ring which sat high on her right hand. 'I see you're wearing a ring. Is it your wedding ring perhaps?'

'No, I bought it for myself in Florence a long time ago. It's a butterfly wing, readying to fly. I liked the symbolism so I still wear it.'

'It's beautiful. It becomes you.'

'The goldsmith said to me it was an opening to a new world.'

FIGURE OF A WOMAN

That night in the cabin Amy challenged herself to continue to dream. To build an edifice of a new life with him. What if the time with Dusty promised more? What if a girl from the city could inspire a man from the bush? She checked how she'd called herself 'girl.' Already she'd adorned Dusty with the features of a man: responsibility wrapped in strength. What she was adorning herself with, were questions still of her place as a woman: having to parade herself with confidence, being given the tick of approval. It didn't sit with who she knew herself to be though, awkward and shy.

She lay in the bath near the fire, the essential oils the retreat had provided, easing her body and mind as she contemplated how she might listen to her own 'essential truth.' But again the voices bubbled to the surface. 'You'd better be quick, the fruit can only ripen for so long.' It was Barry Delany who had caught her unawares in her vulnerability. Dusty was right about the male venom. It pricked when the barb was intentional and Barry Delany must have watched her downfall with Mark, from a distance of opportunity. The thought of him contemplating when to make his move on her made her sicken and cut across the good mood she'd brought back from the river and her time with Dusty.

But then maybe the trading Barry Delany wanted was a similar gamble to how she traded herself, she reasoned. The market was volatile but so was being a woman. Gender was volatile now too. The codes Amy grew up with were being scrambled. Now you could be whatever you chose to be but making the choice was still a lonesome thing. The world didn't shift on its axis that fast and Amy considered that in the end her choice had to come from the rock she held herself to and not one thrown from someone else.

She remembered her mother and father urging her to finish uni. She'd wanted to quit and bury herself away from responsibilities that in the end, she realised, would catch up with her. Her mother had known there'd be no guarantee of a man to catch her when she fell. Even being married didn't inoculate loneliness. She recalled how her parents couldn't adjust as the world moved past them, the digital world distancing them with its acceleration. Amy had tried to help her parents catch up but in the end she left them to their courtyard gardening and the diminishing returns of their isolation.

As she fed more hot water into the bath and eased herself further under, she could feel the pull of the man she had started to meet as an equal. Dusty must have placed this bath here when he was building and she considered the romance of the water and fire in opposition. The fire that was smouldering inside her, since she'd met him only a day before, was continuing to ignite. She imagined his long body in Cabin 4 stretching out to kick over the edge with legs splayed. The thought of his wild self in rhythm with her didn't seem impossible. Her body was full of expectation that any moment he might knock on the door and she'd call him in.

She could hear the voice of her mother in conflict, 'What do you need a man for?' Amy knew there'd been some unspoken hurt in her she couldn't replay. Some confusion in who she projected to the world which couldn't be fulfilled. Amy wondered what the dreams of her mother must have been. She'd often say, 'You have children and nothing else.' Amy had never questioned the life of a woman essentially in service, without room to be what her own desires called for. It didn't seem fair that women were being given a choice today, unlike her mother's world of submission. But in reality, Amy thought, the world today where these choices exist seems less and less to care.

Outside, the wind had come up and Amy could see the latch on the window had cut loose in its push. The timber frame opened inward and Amy felt the rush of cold air which blew the candle out on the edge of the bath. She pulled the towel towards her and stepped from the bath to close the glass. On the veranda across the way Amy could see his shadow moving back and forth across the room inside. She willed him to turn around and see her as she dropped the towel to the ground. See her in her naked self, ready for his coming.

'Had enough of that cake, don't you think? You don't want to put on any more weight.' It was Mark's voice instead. Mark's presence that filled the space and entered the cracks of her mind. She looked down at her body as an alien. 'How has it come to this?' she wondered. 'How can my body be stolen by someone else's craving and disposal in the end?' She stood by the window contemplating her husband's rejection, the line of her body silhouetted by the fire behind. The memory of Mark's disdain prevented her from awakening to the man across the way who'd come to the window to look out. A man who saw the figure of a woman at last in all her fullness.

KINGFISHER FLIGHT

That day, Liam had come to sit beside Eileen at the river with his sketchbook in his hand. He was tall and handsome but fragile too she could tell. She'd been watching him from the time on the plane and she'd been dreaming to herself that maybe this time the man she was looking at was her David. It was in the eyes that she started to get that idea. He told her they were piercing for a story but she saw the shyness too in the contradiction. She thought to herself, 'It's a hard road he's been travellin' 'pon, but I wouldn't like to pry.' When he asked to sit down she'd been sketching the Shannon in her imagination and so she told him of the wild river of her childhood. The kingfishers with wings of blue iridescence and soft orange belly that would follow her along as she canoed down the banks. How she'd found the same bird here at the retreat on the branch across on the other side.

'If I had my canoe, I could play the same game of hide and seek again with them now.'

'We could ask Dusty if he has one you can use.'

Liam said he could see Eileen though going over the rapids further down and thought maybe it was best that they find a quieter part of the river to travel on. He said that Beth had spoken about the meandering of the river on the flats where she and Sergio had a farm. 'If there was time away from the weekend, we could maybe find the best place to go in but I guess if a weekend is all we've got it doesn't make much sense.' He was solemn then as if he didn't want this time to end. Eileen wanted to reassure him though that she had other thoughts.

'Well, I've been thinkin' I'll stay on a wee bit longer, ye see. I'm not done yet with this place, or maybe it's just not done with me at all.' Liam was staring into Eileen then and thought he could paint her like that, suspended in an awakening solitude.

And then he took a chance to say the words she needed to hear to finally let the pain go. 'I wonder, Eileen, if you might be lonely. Is that what brings you here?' Eileen held still for a moment, assessing whether he was looking to write a story about her or whether he might be willing to break her confidence and all. But then he reached out and held her hand. She knew the touch from somewhere, a vulnerability mixed with strength. It was a touch she'd felt in David before he caught that plane to go to war. She clutched at the young man as if he was her David. He didn't pull away though, until she signalled it was safe at last to let go.

'It's OK, Eileen. I understand.'

And then the tears really flowed and she told him about her lost boy and how she'd been to the Sorry speech for forced adoptions in parliament. About the women, who were lined along the seats crying and the politicians trying to free their guilt.

'But the women, ye see, can't forget. We had no power then, and we've no power now. I let my boy go because I thought it was for the best, but I was wrong.'

She told him of the women who had a pillow put before their eyes and never saw their baby at all but she had held her son until they came with a needle to silence her.

'Given a chance, I could've made it work.'

And then her whole body became a Picasso weeping woman. There was no shame in the weeping and she could see that it was time for the tears to come. He waited beside her while the pain broke, her hand in his. She hadn't come to this place before where the time for crying was real. The kingfisher was diving in a streak of blue and the fish in its beak flapped sideways as it fed it to its young. It was a biological urging she was thinking. She could hear her son knocking on some far away door trying to be heard and she only needed for him to know that she was here, listening … waiting. They sat together by the river and it was like there was some special understanding they were having between them and she wondered, 'Who is this young man beside me now?'

Then the other woman, Amy, broke the moment they were

having and even though Eileen wasn't ready, she turned to Amy instead and let her in. Amy liked Eileen's drawing and made some remark and then she asked for Liam to reveal himself. He hesitated at first and seemed to ask Eileen's permission and then he showed them both the work that he'd be doing and Eileen could have cried at the beauty of it. Amy was so impressed and Eileen saw him blush and put it away. But Eileen had seen the light he'd captured on the water and the elegant line of trees which made their way to the ridgeline. And there, in the far corner of the drawing, was the flight of the kingfisher like an arrow into the stream.

That night around the fire, Beth asked them for their stories. When it was his turn, Liam told them of his mother and father who had died. He spoke about feeling lost and adrift and how he'd been taught to live with uncertainty and now his upbringing was coming home to test him. He spoke about the paper and the story he was after and he looked to Amy Bentley who turned away. Eileen wondered what her connection to him could be. Beth said that on Easter Sunday they were to have a ritual gathering in the woods and to be up at dawn for the service. Eileen studied Liam's hands as he sat listening quietly. Folded together under the chin, they were the hands of contemplation, she thought. Easter seemed to be a special time for other reasons besides the cross. It was then Eileen realised her own hands were in mirror image to his, his right hand revealing a sign she'd missed before.

When he left for the cabin that night, Eileen stood at the main house as if she'd seen a ghost. There was no goodbye in her and she thought she could go even deeper if she thought it could be safe. Their time at the river held a moment of comfort and he had said he would like to write about her if Eileen gave him her permission. He said she could be one of those stories of loss that the government was recognising. But a seat in a parliamentary sitting wasn't going to heal the trauma of the past. She thought that some places people are drawn to for healing. The Retreat was becoming such a place.

Eileen tried to gather her sense about the pieces that were aligning. Was it a coincidence that the moments she'd been with him had brought a hope she'd dare not reveal even to herself? And yet the questions kept coming about the way he looked, his eyes, his touch and now the final piece, the birthmark on his right hand. How was it possible that a dream could come true in a simple place at the beginning of a stream? A stream that even now was rushing to the ocean in a push of giving birth.

DISCOVERING DAVID

Eileen came to the door of Dusty's cabin after the others had left the main house and the session for the night. She'd waited in the dark outside and could see the man inside pacing the room in some kind of agitation. Inside Dusty sat confused. His time with Amy was unexpected and now he considered over the past few days how Eileen was coming home to the place. He'd watched as she and Liam were establishing a bond. He could see in the way they got together on the retreat, that she was recognising a longing that was becoming real. Her figure in the doorway was composed, as if she had risen to face what he had to say.

Eileen was direct and urgent now in how she looked at Dusty as he rose to greet her, as if the words he had to tell her could not wait. 'I know y're Dusty – that Liam and Amy have spoken about – but we've yet to meet properly. Is there a reason y're keepin' yer distance from me?'

'Come in, Eileen, and I'll make you a cup of tea. I have a few things to explain but you'll need to sit down I think.' He took her arm and led her to the fire where she sat with a patience that had been a lifetime coming. He'd come between people's lives at a delicate point and he didn't know if the reality of another person's dreams was too much for him to bare.

'Was the letter in the mail deliberate then? Was I meant to be here an' all?'

The hope that Dusty saw rising in her was being drawn from a deep well that she had all but buried. He didn't want to harm her but the process of unravelment had begun when Dusty had discovered who she was and had set out on the journey to find her. Jack had been insistent, 'Find her, Dusty, and bring all that I have left of David home to me.' He weighed the implications of starting something that would become a flood which couldn't be resisted. What he had to say to Eileen was being carried in a boat of hope that needed now to reach the shore.

'Eileen, I have news from the past and I have something that I hope is your future.' He passed her the tea and they sat together as the fire flickered up. He didn't quite know why but they sat staring into the coals for a while, until he could find the words to speak. The breath between them was suspended until Dusty could feel a rhythm that belonged to them both. It was as if she now was guiding him, in the task of uncovering the truth by her silence.

'First I need to tell you the story of Old Jack who owns this place that I helped to build. Jack has had to come to reconcile himself and his grief in this place. His family are all but lost and he has had to hold fast to a dream. He had a dream you see, to bring people here for healing, just like he has had to try to heal himself after he lost his wife and son. He believes that we come from nature and we go back to nature in the end. He wanted to help people discover who they truly are by experiencing themselves as part of that nature that we all long for.'

'An' who is it now I'm meant to be discovering here? D'ye know?'

Dusty looked at her vulnerability that was turning to strength as she asked the question she'd never dared to ask until now. He prayed his plan would work and he began to simply state the truth. He had seen the way they'd come together as friends first. The way they had settled into the valley and found a part of themselves that was missing. Now it was time for them to find their true identity at last.

'You are the woman, Eileen, who Jack's son fell in love with. You are the woman, David had said he intended to marry when he returned from Vietnam.'

And then the years lifted away and Dusty saw the young woman whom David must have met, before he took that fateful journey. He saw her eyes go to a place that she was sharing with someone else and he saw a tender awakening there. He imagined her meeting the young soldier for the first time, his eyes brightly lit on her instead of the war he was going to. She looked to Dusty and then away, as if to thread the time of loss between then and now.

'But sure how d'ye know for certain it's my David we're talkin' about? I need to know, y'see. I need not to be lost again.' There was a power in her now, a power of redemption Dusty was seeing. It was as if David had risen to stand beside her. What Dusty could see would bring David home to Jack, but also was bringing Eileen home to herself at last.

'He loved you, Eileen. My dad was with him in Vietnam. He told my dad about the woman who served him perfume at the counter in DJ's and gave him the love he needed to face what he was going into. They were mates and Dad never got over the guilt that it was David who was shot and not him. Dad said David had pushed him down and taken the bullet in the chest himself. If it wasn't for Jack who was able to accept and give Dad comfort, I don't think Dad would have recovered from the nightmares that plagued our family for years. Dad sent me here to help Jack build the retreat and when Jack found out about you, he sent me to find you.'

'And where is this Jack? Does he know I'm here at all?'

'We're meeting him in the morning. He has a place further back in the forest that we're heading to at dawn. He knows you're here and he cannot wait to meet you. You see, Eileen, you are the only one Jack had left until now.' He was awkward in how to bring the next moment of revelation to light. It was good news, the best news but how to deliver it with dignity was what he knew it deserved.

She'd come to his door because there was something about Liam she needed answering and now she was holding the truth of the man she loved in her grasp. 'But why have ye left it this long? Sure why didn't I meet Jack and yerself when I arrived?' She looked confused and shaken and Dusty didn't know if it was right to tell her now or wait until the morning.

'We wanted to let you feel the place first, become part of the place where David was raised. I'd convinced Jack it was for the best because I wanted you to meet the other person who is on the retreat with you first.' At that moment a gasp arose and she clutched at her belly as the force deepened. She got up and moved to steady herself against the hearth, staring down into the coals that danced to tell their stories.

Dusty came close to her and reached out to hold her hand. She responded with instinct but where her mind had entered into, Dusty had no way to tell. He spoke gently then as if in the unravelling, a thread could not be lost. 'Eileen, Jack hasn't met Liam either.' She turned to face him, a look of wonder in her eyes now. A look that bent the bars of the prison she'd lain in for forty years.

'I think you might be starting to understand who he really is, Eileen.' The words were not his. They belonged to Eileen. They belonged to David who touched the young Irish woman with his love. They belonged to Jack who was waiting in the woods for their return.

Her back was to him now so that in the uncovering, her place was hers alone. 'I saw the spark in his eyes that I've known before. Is that what y're tellin' me? Sure don't go tellin' me somethin' that's not true.' She was still now, as still as one of those flitches under the surface of the water that was being brought back to life.

And then Dusty brought the name home to her. The name she'd held in her heart and had never let go. 'Eileen, Liam David Patterson is your son, David.'

He expected her to collapse but what he could see instead was how her shoulders lifted, lifted to carry the good news of her son. She got up slowly then and went to the window and looked towards the cabin Liam was occupying. She turned to Dusty as if he had delivered her baby to her again but this time there were no walls or needles to come between. 'The lights are out. So he must be sleepin' now. I will wait Dusty. I will wait till morning.'

'Eileen, Jack doesn't know he has a grandson. I want you to be the one to tell him yourself.' She nodded then and came towards

Dusty until her head was on his chest and the sobbing began. He held her softly and stroked her hair for all the pain she had endured. 'It's OK, Eileen, forgive me. I didn't know any other way to tell you. And now I need your help to tell Old Jack.'

'Does he know who I am?'

'I'm afraid not, Eileen. I brought him here to help with the mine threat and when I found you at last, I found out about him being your son by accident.'

'How d'ye mean now?'

'When I found your employment records through the David Jones archives, I was able to trace your time of leaving and where you went to after. The address at the presbytery gave me the idea of the possibility of why you were there. It happened to other girls at the time and I thought why not you? So I followed the story and found out that you had delivered a baby boy who was adopted out. The presbytery had the records and when I found out your David had been given the name Liam David Patterson, I knew that name from the papers. I was already in touch with him.'

FOREST MEETING

Dusty had said that Old Jack wanted to meet them and make them breakfast. But Jack was an early riser, so they'd need to leave at dawn to be at his place that was back up the ridge a bit, he'd added. For Liam it was a difficult Easter Sunday morning on his fortieth birthday with no-one back home to share it with. The Retreat was a good place to bury the expectation, he rationalised. Easter eggs were in the past too, as was Mass that he used to attend with his mum and dad in Randwick. His dad would kneel at the cross at the back of the church as they'd wait for him in the car. He said he was doing his penance for the sins he hadn't let go. But on Liam's birthday there had always been presents for their son. His parents, he knew, had loved him deeply and he missed them.

As they gathered outside the cabins, the morning chill had already settled in. There was a fog further down the valley but up at The Retreat, the air was clear and blue. Liam was looking forward to meeting the old man whom Dusty had spoken about with such respect. 'They're Jack's ideas you see. He just needed help to realise them.' Dusty had explained that Jack was concerned for the health of the people and the valley. The threat of mining was too real. Apparently, it was Jack who had urged Dusty to phone the paper about mining leases overriding farmers' rights.

'It needs a city voice,' Jack had urged. 'That Liam Patterson seems to have his head screwed on the right way.' Dusty had said Jack kept up with the latest news online and Liam took it as a compliment that Jack had recognised his work.

Now they were being led through the bush to his home. Amy Bentley was in close step behind Dusty. Liam noticed how she'd changed in the past few days. Her hair hung loose and her green dress was left unbuckled to swirl at her ankles casually. He noticed her absorbed in how the downward flow of sunlight penetrated the forest as the sun rose higher. She looked happy and Liam thought that whatever her situation was back home, she looked like she had grown beyond it.

She whispered excitedly, 'A brush turkey. Look!' Her hemline was gathered around her as she moved off the path and through the bush to get a better look at the blue-black body and the bare red head.

Dusty followed to stand close beside her. 'It's domestic, you know. It sweeps the leaves and builds a mound to house the eggs for the female.' He swung his focus back to Eileen and Liam who were left behind on the path. 'The young have to fend for themselves when they hatch but the instinct is there for them to survive.' He turned back then to pause and watch the bird which ignored their presence, its yellow throat wattle hanging limply as it foraged.

'Looks like the animal world seems to get it then,' Liam quipped. There must be something natural in the way we're meant to grow. I'm not sure why we humans get it so wrong.'

'It's a mystery to me too, Mate. Maybe we've just forgotten what it is to be real.' Dusty had thrown the remark over his shoulder as he got onto his knees beside Amy who seemed mesmerised.

'Well, this is real to me.' Liam was patting the tree with the smooth pink bark at the top, which stood beside the path. 'I know this one. It's a brush box.' Liam recognised the species which had lined his street in Sydney, planted because of its resilience. 'I remember how I used to hang by my knees and swing off from its branches. I used to try to make the world right by seeing it upside down.' He smiled at Eileen. 'Maybe that's what drew me to journalism, an urge to find the truth and add my perspective to it.'

'Were you all alone then, I wonder?'

'Was I an only child do you mean, Eileen?'

'Sure, I shouldn't be askin' now. I'm sorry.'

'No, that's fine, Eileen. I had no brothers and sisters but I had a loving family and that's all that mattered.'

'Fer sure, you were lucky then.'

Her eyes went down and Liam noticed her usual spark was gone. 'Come on, Eileen. I'm sure this visit to Jack will hold some surprises. What do you say, Dusty? Not long now?'

'Just about there.'

As they turned the corner, Dusty stopped at the bridge which led to Jack's place. In the morning light, it sat in a clearing with spider webs glistening silver in the grass. Jack's dog ran to him and Dusty bent to pat him like an old friend. 'Good boy, Joe.'

'Hey Dusty, I thought you'd said it was a shack.' Liam liked the cabin that looked warm and well-built, the aroma of baking bread wafting from its interior to entice him.

'I didn't say Jack was a hobo,' Dusty grinned.

'Who you calling hobo, Son?'

Jack had come to the door with an excitement in his eyes. He was strong and rugged and even though he was old, his back was straight like steel. His hands were cracked with years of hard work and Liam thought he'd done well to survive out here in isolation.

'Sorry, Jack. Just a city misunderstanding,' Dusty laughed.

'Well, welcome to my home then. I've been waiting a long time to meet my guests.'

Surprisingly, his voice was vibrant as if the boy in the man was dominant. However, he paused then and went into silence as if he had no more to say. He looked past the rest and his eyes settled on the woman he'd been waiting for.

'So it's Eileen is it?

'Yes, Jack. I been waitin' a lifetime t'meet you, at last.'

Jack surveyed her, as if he was seeing someone else or maybe someone else standing beside her. Liam watched in confusion as Eileen stood still, her head bent. It seemed she was waiting for approval. Then, an awkward silence which Liam didn't think right to break. Something was going on. Dusty had led them to Eileen's simple words 'at last' but Liam had no idea how he was the final answer.

Dusty stood beside Liam and tried to explain. 'Jack and Eileen have a special bond. You see, Eileen loved Jack's son. He was tragically killed in the Vietnam War and the promised marriage never happened.' Liam looked towards Eileen and Jack who seemed oblivious to anything but each other for the moment. Then just before Eileen went inside, she looked back to him with a recognition in her eyes. A longing he couldn't decipher. Through the window, Liam could see Jack showing Eileen something that seemed precious as they sat together by the fire. She was gently stroking what looked like a photograph in a frame.

Dusty, on the other hand, was beginning to shake. It was as if he was finally giving up a baton that had been passed to him, which he could now release. Liam tried to assist. 'Do you want to sit down, Mate? You don't look so well.'

Then Amy intervened. 'Are you OK, Dusty? Their held glance made Liam feel like he was looking in on a drama that was playing out before him. He then saw Jack come to the window and Jack's stunned gaze was on him. What was the story that was unfolding, he wondered? The melodrama was palpable but no-one seemed to be laughing.

Jack then came onto the veranda. 'Um, I wanted to invite you all here this morning to help recreate a memory for me.' He stalled and cleared his throat. 'I hope also for you to take a memory away with you. I knew Eileen was here at the retreat and I wanted to meet her for the first time and share a gift with her. I invited you along as my witnesses. But now … now I am beginning to see there is more than I could ever have imagined taking place.' Jack stilled then and Eileen came and put her arm through his. He directed his words towards her. 'I would like you to come to the bridge where there is something special I'd like to show you.'

The bridge was a simple log construction over a tumble of rock and water. A natural bowl held the spill-over of water coming down from the hills. The rock held mottled leaves in the bottom which stirred as the water funnelled into it in a child's waterfall.

'David and I built this bridge together when he was little. Underneath it was David's favourite place to come and play. He used to say that the fairies must have built it to wash all our cares away. I know it's a simple thing but I would like us all to take it in turns to stand in the stream and cleanse our feet.' Jack paused then and turned to Liam with a direct look of anticipation. 'What do you say, Son? Would you go first?'

Eileen and Jack stood on the bank and watched as Liam took off his runners and entered the water. Amy stood back with Dusty. It was as if Liam was the main event. The water was colder after the night of frost they'd had. The water came to his knees and as the bowl emptied and filled with the rush of water, Liam saw below the waterline, the name 'David' carved on the side.

'Hey, there's a name here, Jack. Do you know who carved it?'

Jack looked at Liam with an unrecognisable sorrow. Then Liam remembered Dusty's reporting of how Jack had lost his son tragically. Liam had nothing to offer him that might relieve the pain of memory he was so obviously experiencing but he tried to lighten the moment anyway. 'It's my middle name too, you know.' He hesitated then to assert himself, deciding that the time to speak up was now. 'Oh, and it's my birthday today. I'm forty.'

Jack and Eileen clung to each other. 'Well, how about we sing Happy Birthday to you then, Son. Eileen, how about you lead the singing of Happy Birthday to David.'

It's at those moments in time that come to you like in a dream, that hold a promise for who you can eventually become. Jack had dreamed of helping others. He had risen above the losses and held that calm acceptance which he knew was all that any of us could do in the end. All that he could control was inside himself and now things outside his control were being drawn into that small space in the woods. They sat by the fire and Jack brought out the albums that until now had held only the past, the one at Boat Beach a special surprise for Eileen. 'I know this place. We went there together.'

Liam's grandfather sighed with an understanding. 'The beach is at the end of this valley, Eileen. It's where the waters from here enter the sea.' He looked to Eileen and tightened the grip on her hand. 'David was bringing you home then, Eileen. He must have wanted you to know his territory before he went away. '

'That weekend, I remember him looking towards the western hills as if there was some place special he knew and I asked him. He said he would take me there in time but this time was ours and he wanted me all for himself.'

'Yes, that sounds like David. He knew what was important and what to let go.'

Liam's mother was sharing something beyond the family history, something Jack was holding himself still to hear. 'He showed me the cave he used to hang out in and the shell middens. He said that Aborigines had been there way before him and that the place needed to be respected. He wanted me to understand what this place meant to him. He said it was the place he went to, to find his own identity.'

'Yes, a father needs a son to find his own way. I didn't begrudge him that. It was David who said I needed to stop cutting down the trees. I got the idea in the end but it was too late.' Jack was holding the egg he'd carved and he held his hand out to Liam. 'I carved this for Mary. It's yours now. I'd like you to have it for your birthday.' The timber was warm in Liam's hand as it transferred across from grandfather to grandson. It was Easter and the egg had been delivered from an unexpected hand.

WOODEN BOX

David's things were inside a wooden box Jack had brought out for Liam and Eileen to see. Dusty had led Amy outside to wait, the family time was for a private memory.

'He made it at school. He was proud to bring it home.' The box was big enough for a small boy to stand on. Eileen was imagining David dragging it to the window of the home he grew up in, the locked up house that sat outside the retreat. A house she hoped one day to enter. David had told her that from his bedroom window, he could reach up to touch the sky.

'Where did he keep it, Jack?' Eileen was retracing, capturing David as a boy, bringing her experience of love into stronger focus.

'Under his bed.' He coughed as the words became real. 'He said, when he was a little boy, that the fairies like the dark places to rest.' Jack was resisting what he had not understood of David's character when he was growing up. The mystery of David was held with Mary who had read the children's book of Peter Pan to him every night until he had tucked it in the box and finally sealed the lid. Jack lifted the worn book from the box and an image of a boy with a sword surfaced. 'He said he used to dream that he could fly, like Peter. I worried that Mary was putting nonsense in his head but now I don't know what to believe anymore.'

'What are these, Jack?' Liam had pulled out a set of wooden insects with helicopter wings.

'These are the dragonflies he loved to watch on the river. He could spend hours observing them and he had a go at making some from the flitches. That's where I got the idea to do the same. He said that dragonflies were just like Peter in the way they hovered lightly and could fly backwards.'

Jack sat quietly with a child's dragonfly in his hand. A rough stick with wings pieced together with string.

'How old was he then, Jack?' Eileen was looking into the memory of David. She pictured the boy inside the man who had walked away into a war where children's swords could not protect him.

'He was seven when he gave it up. A girl from school laughed at him.' Jack sat on the edge of his bed and stared at the woman who had given birth to his grandson. 'Tell me, do you understand why a boy would believe in fairy tales?'

Liam watched as Jack sat unsure of the past. 'Were you close, Jack?' He was gently persuading Jack to let go himself, let go of the questions he had been unable to reconcile. Questions of how to make a man out of a boy who would never grow up.

'I was rough. I treated him too roughly. To try and show him how to face the world … but I was wrong. Boys don't become men just by being strong. It has to come with being gentle with yourself first. That's what I've learnt now. That's what Mary taught me.'

He pulled out the last of the objects from the box. A fading photograph of a grinning boy with pants rolled up as he waded into the river. 'That's him catching dragonflies on his finger. He wouldn't hurt them. He just liked to make the connection. That's all.'

'That's what I felt when I met him, Jack. That's why I fell in love with him so quickly. I needn't have asked why.' Eileen was smiling, bringing back the memory of a man in uniform who walked into the department store and into her life forever.

'You were right to trust him. He was a good boy. He would have made a good husband to you.'

'I've always known that. We just didn't get the chance.' She turned to Liam then who held her gaze. The three strangers sat quietly together until their distance lessened as they recognised a connection.

'You taught him right, Jack. I wished I'd known him. But maybe we can get to know each other now. David would have wanted that I'm sure. I think I might stick around here some more.

Dusty said that you'd like me to do a few paintings and write a few stories to help out. I thought I might start with that old house further down the river. It's already in some of my landscapes.'

Jack stared at Liam as if the naming of the house, the house he had locked away supposedly for good, had suddenly gained form and substance simply by it being acknowledged. 'No need to go there just yet. We'll get to know each other first I think.' His mind, once trapped in the memory of a family who were lost to him, was beginning to open.

Outside by the bridge, Amy could see through the cabin window to the family inside. She watched as Jack boiled the kettle and Eileen helped with the pancakes, cracking the eggs into the mixture to be stirred by Jack. The pan was held above the fire and Amy watched as Jack carefully poured the mixture in, Eileen flipping the cooked pancakes onto the plate for Liam to coat with lemon and sugar. He had already started to eat before the rest of the group, just like a child would do. It was a first for all of them. Liam was being fed by Jack like a little rescued bird, rolling the pancake into a tube to eat easily with the hands, Eileen standing back to watch.

Outside, Amy watched Dusty patching the rock face with David's name inscribed on the inside. 'The flood broke some of the rock away but it can be fixed.' Dusty wedged pieces of rock into one side of the bowl that had splintered. 'Now it can fill up properly.'

He was meticulous. Each piece of rock was carefully chosen and placed just as he had made the seat on the ridge. Amy watched as the little pebbles were given as much weight of consideration as the bigger pieces. She thought about the firm back in Sydney, her desk piled high with the big things of finance which wouldn't wait for someone who was more expendable the longer she was away. Where value lay was in the mind's eye, she knew. It was as if the world had been propelled down a track of excess, where to halt your trajectory was to lose your advantage. And yet pausing here was the opposite. Here to stop meant her breath could be felt at last. And in that breath came the flush of desire.

'I'm going to bathe my feet too.' She kept her back to him as if she knew he was to consider her. Consider how she picked her way across the scramble of rocks, barefoot. Yes, she knew he was observing. Observing the way she left her jacket folded on the rocks as a marker. The way she lifted her dress with a mischief.

THE WAY I FEEL

That night Dusty took Amy to the waterhole again. Amy considered how the day had changed her completely. Dusty had trusted her to be there while Eileen, Jack and Liam came together as a family. They'd walked to the top of the ridge where Dusty had been building the lookout. The coast was discernible in the distance. Separate entrances to the sea split from the delta and Jack had pointed to the furthest one south that Boat Beach sat near. Closest to Sydney. Closer for David to have taken Eileen away for that solitary weekend together. Dusty had carried up the plaque Jack wanted to be placed on the top. The simple words, 'Be gentle with yourself,' were carved into one of the flitches of a red cedar cutting.

It was a symbolic act but Amy watched as Dusty took the words and placed them on the top of the rock shelf he had built. She knew that this man would not hold her in submission like Mark had. This man was kind. Whatever else their future might hold, it would be different. She was different now, falling for a man who valued himself as well as the environment. She was willing to stay on at the retreat until a plan could be worked out to help Jack and his family as well as Dusty.

She thought of Barry Delany and the dirt he had on Mark. Could she confront Mark? Could she threaten to expose his actions? She didn't think so. She couldn't spend one more moment with a snake like Barry Delany, for any reason. From her time at the retreat came a self-respect that she wouldn't compromise. She realised Mark hadn't stolen her love. She'd given it away. Now she was seeing that her love was part of who she was, not what Mark had taken for granted.

He sat on the water's edge with his head down and Amy saw a shyness there she knew was in her as well. She approached him carefully.

'You did the right thing, Dusty. It was a shock I think for everyone but there was no easy way to bring together all that loss and find a place for it to settle.'

From the outside of the group, Amy could see that shifting people's lives to a new reality, was a matter of taking care. There were no guarantees that everyone would accept the relationships. She wasn't sure if Dusty was thinking about a relationship with her but she knew what she wanted and decided to act on it. She remembered the yearning from last night, the touch of her skin opening up to pleasure she hoped might be returned.

'I like the way I feel here, Dusty. I like spending time with you.' She was taking a chance with this open admission but she was prepared for whatever outcome was there. Amy needed to express herself clearly. Maybe for the first time. Maybe that girl who couldn't make herself heard or understood was at last able to speak for herself.

'You're not going back, Amy, … are you?' The question held between them as Dusty searched for the recognition that she had forgiven him. He'd taken advantage of her and in so doing he'd lost self-respect. You can't harm another without a part of you being lost too. 'You know, I'd really like you to stay on, not just because of your old ties with the law firm.' Dusty was struggling. He had been pre-occupied, but there was something about this woman. She didn't presume. She was simply herself. But he knew in reality it was really the desire that had been building since he'd seen her by the window last night, a desire that he was caught in, in its inevitable embrace.

At first, Amy hadn't read the signs he was sending. She reassured him she had already been considering what she could do away from Sydney. She'd been thinking of an idea that might just help the valley solve its problems. But it was not the time for that now. The river was urging past in a flow that began to melt into her. She saw the strength of his body as the moon lit up his profile. The reflection in his eyes that questioned was she ready. It had been too long and now the time and the place was right. The unpeeling of the layers was already happening and there was no turning back. Not now. In her too, there was only the desire to stay.

Then Dusty took her in his arms and kissed her. The trees behind were lit up with stars that made it look like Christmas. His mouth was warm and his tongue entered into her. Gently. She pulled into his body and they began to move like lovers. Slowly, surely. His mouth was searching. Her back arched in reply. He led her then to a grove between the trees. The grass was flattened here and he lay her down on his jacket. It had been some time for him too and he wasn't sure. Wasn't sure of what opening up so suddenly would mean.

PEACE ROSE

The river was wider on the flats. Dairy properties and small scale farming had produced a mixed ensemble of residents which had grown to match the overspill from the city. Some of the farmers had swapped to tourism and country properties were becoming favourite places for children from the city to learn where their food actually came from. It was like a reverse Easter Show with displays of city folk in their four wheel drives, burning up the dirt road to the markets which were held in the showground.

'So, what do you think they'll make of us, Jack? Your family might be a talking point, don't you think?' Amy was worried that her presence in the community could challenge some. She had a proposal to help maximize profits for the locals rather than the mining companies. The profits meant more than money. It included the ecosystem as the first premise.

'Don't worry about the locals. But watch ... the slower they talk, the shrewder they are. They'll size you up, no doubt about it but what's there to be worried about?' Jack had a self-belief that came from a lifetime of honest hard work. Amy, on the other hand, was growing into a recognition of who she was, as she learnt to nurture Mary's roses back to life and help provide organic food for weekend residents who continued to come to the retreat for renewal. A bucket of Peace roses were at her feet in the van. The yellow centre blushed pink at the edges and subtly perfumed the van.

'I'm grateful to you, Amy.' Jack smiled in the rear view mirror at Amy who sat with Dusty and Liam in the back seat.

'For what, Jack? It's me who should thank you.'

'Those roses were left to rot beside the house. I couldn't even look at them when she died but now ... now they don't just remind me of Mary, they give me Mary back.'

Dusty squeezed Amy's hand and she looked past a lifetime of

self-doubt. 'Things grow well here, Jack.'

'It's in the water, they say.' Jack was pensive as he sat beside Eileen who looked across the fields newly planted with Lucerne. He smiled sideways at Eileen as he kept one eye on the dirt road. 'It's David's stomping ground, Eileen.'

'Did he play here too?' Her eyes widened to take in all the corners of David's life. She'd been to the house where he grew up, all locked away. The decking boards had split in the sun. Dusty was quietly replacing the entrance step and handrails for the time Jack was ready to enter again. Amy had dug up the roses there and replanted them at the retreat. Eileen suspected though that Jack must have realised the steady rebuilding taking place.

'Sun up to sun down when he was older. He could be anywhere. Run wild he did. Mary and I were concerned but he never got into any trouble that we knew about. It was hard to let go after he was lost once.'

The others looked towards Jack for an explanation but Dusty's glance silenced them with a warning look as Jack went suddenly quiet. Talking about Mary and David was difficult but seemed to complete the family now that racketed over the timber bridge and into the gates of the showground. As the van pulled up before the ticket seller on the gate, Jack sat quietly with his hands on the steering wheel.

'You OK, Jack?' From the back seat, Dusty had his hand gently now on Jack's shoulder easing the tension there.

'You know she planted the Peace Rose after David died. She said we needed to show that the war wouldn't defeat us completely.' He looked towards Eileen who was sitting beside him.

'It's alright, Jack. We'll be doing our best to look after you now.'

'I'm hoping we'll look after each other, Eileen. What do you say?' But then he was doubting in the change that had happened too quickly. Doubting that the journey they'd been on for the past six months to create a new family could be real. His grandson sat in the back seat. Eileen had baked bread with Jack and the time they'd spent together had taught him that being alone was a penance he didn't need anymore. Dusty had found Amy and they were good for each other.

Liam reached forward over the front seat and kissed his grandfather on the back of the head. 'Come on, Grandad, let's get this show on the road.' Jack held himself still and Eileen beside him, kissed him on the cheek. He dropped his head then as Dusty and Amy reached over to hold onto him as well. How a group of individuals had come to his rescue was beyond him.

Jack wiped his eyes with his shirt sleeve. It was a silent time that had settled into him and then suddenly, as if the young Jack still had momentum, he bounced back. 'Yea, well you motley bunch will need to get out there and start selling. We've got a big day ahead of us.'

'OK, old man.'

'Who you calling old, Dusty? You better watch your place.'

'My place is just where I want it, Jack. You can be sure of that.'

THE MARKET

The market was buzzing with ordered chaos. Stalls were half set up with umbrellas to protect the people and the produce from the sun. A guitarist was plugging into the sound system and testing the mic. Banners were being erected that publicised a race to raise money for the local school. Their spot was beside Beth and Sergio in the artisan section. Artworks of all kinds and abilities were on display but because of his reputation, people knew to visit for Sergio's sculptures. The work he had on display was soothing. Water sculptures spilled increasing intensities of sound over edges of stones, as water which had filled the vessel, trickled away to emptiness. It reminded Amy of the stone bowl under the bridge with David's name carved in it. Holding the rhythms of flow. Jack and Dusty set their stall up with 'The Retreat' signage that Liam had painted. It included a winding river of gold that threaded its way through the valley. His paintings lined up on one side, Jack's figures of abstract shapes were on the other and the produce from the garden and home baked breads sat alongside Mary's roses. They were self-sufficient and operating in a self-made economy that took a community of like-minded people to flourish in.

Sam, the guitarist, was joined by a young woman singer with curly red hair that lit up with sunlight. Her voice was round and full and sure of its musicianship. 'That's Melanie, Beth and Sergio's daughter. She writes her own lyrics and Sam, her friend from school, composes the music. They have a unique sound don't you think … a mix of jazz with a funky beat.' Dusty was introducing Amy to the locals through the connections, pointing to and explaining each group of people who had been invited to the meeting later that day. 'The Davidsons are working on a solar project and the Bianchis are using that system for pizza baking.' The smell of fresh garlic and olives had already brought a line to form as had the local coffee roaster, River Windings Organic

Coffee, owned by the McCaffreys.

Jack was beating some timber sticks on the bench in time with the music, the years falling from him as his boyish enthusiasm continued to surface. Dusty pulled Amy from the stall to dance with him. Her embarrassment turned to pleasure as a group of people stood around and clapped them on. She hadn't danced like this, since before she was married. Dusty was kicking the dust up as an accompaniment and Amy just held on and swung around and into the patterns of movement he was creating. All she had to do was go his way and the earth spun under her as she was lifted into the air. Amy was having fun, dancing for the sake of being outrageous and silly and altogether in love with this gorgeous man who was holding her and not letting her go. She looked to the stall and saw Liam with his arm around his mum who couldn't hold back her smile.

The man from the gallery in Sydney approached, carefully dressed in neutral tones to blend in. The tailoring was a giveaway though. No-one else at the market had such luxury, not that it was a priority when everyday living was all they could manage. Amy had been talking to Jack and Liam about the possibilities and they had decided on a plan of action. There was more opportunity when people came together. Sergio had agreed as well and the Valley Artists Inc. had been born.

'I see you've expanded your operations, Jack. What's this signage for?' He examined Liam's work. The illuminated gold river in the signage was original and evocative. He'd need to make sure he secured that artist as well but now was the time for first business principles: smile and put the client at ease. 'Great day in the country, Jack. Been busy? What have you got for me today?' His eyes darted eagerly over the merchandise while his casual demeanour obscured his intent for a cheap purchase.

'You'll have to talk to my manager this time. Amy Bentley meet Brandon Savage.' Jack smirked, enjoying the back step Brandon took as he gave Amy the once over.

She took control, Jack nodding his approval. She knew that the people in the valley needed her capacity to represent them. 'If you're interested in any of the works here for sale, we can do a deal for your gallery if you wish but we'll need to offer you a contract for a commission, for goods on consignment.'

Amy had already negotiated with other artists in the valley that the best way to have a powerful profile was to band together. They were going to need all the power they could get. The meeting that night would determine their future. Bartering with the gallery owner was the first step. Brandon Savage paused. His easy agency was over. Now he had to deal with a group who were far better informed. He'd have liked to walk away and show he didn't desire what they had to offer but there were already orders in from his clients. Even with his profit margin shrinking, he knew the decision needed to be sealed. The risk was another gallery finding their way up the valley. Besides the work of Liam Patterson was extraordinary, with the light captured in the mirroring off the water.

'Well, I'll need to see a contract then.'

Amy already had one drawn up and to his surprise it was detailed and waterproof. She was meticulous. The artists were in business for something far more worthwhile than money. What they were selling was an identity that had value far beyond their own individual names on canvas and sculptures. These were the Valley Artists. People who expressed the land and themselves as part of it. To them it was indivisible. They wanted the knowledge to be conveyed to the buyer that the land was their signature, the whole of it and not piecemeal.

He was sweating now and confused even. What kind of enterprise was on offer which required him to sell for a collective and not just an individual? Amy assured him he had a cooling off period but he said that no, he could take some of the works back now and come back in a few weeks for some more.

'Oh, and one thing more. We've been putting together a special exhibition and we'd like you to promote us as a whole group. Dusty has a studio built for a resident artist to come up so we'd be happy for you to promote that too.' Amy was giving him the full intention of the artists to be recognised and testing his capacity to be on their side.

'Well, you've done your homework then.' He paused and his eyes looked to the ground in calculation. Was he capable of representing them and their vision? Amy hoped. Maybe something other than financial opportunity had brought him to the valley. Was the valley and its people capable of wooing interest and so shift the dominant city approach to art? It needed to, if they were to survive and the country thrive. She watched him look around at the locals who were happily bartering, children calmly playing, the river winding through. Then Jack came over and held a set of the prayers beads, he usually made for friends, out to him.

'I'd like to give you a gift, Mr Savage.' They're made from river stone and the inscription on the medal attached, is for you especially.'

He turned them in his hands and the inscription on the medal, 'Be gentle with yourself,' became visible. His shoulders dropped then and a tension, Amy had seen him carrying as a landmark, eased.

'Thank you, Jack. Your work has served me well. They can't get enough of your reborn flitches in Double Bay. You might add some more of these beads in as well.'

'These beads aren't for sale. I give them away to friends and those who need it.'

'I think we all need it, Jack.' The gallery owner then took in the community around him again. He'd kept coming up to the valley for the bargains but it was also the beauty of the work, he realised. It took a special something to create a beauty that couldn't be manufactured. It had to do with the soul of the place. 'And I think I can manage that exhibition but I'll need the details of what you intend to exhibit. The Opera House forecourt would be as good as any place. What do you think? Do you think you could manage that? At New Year?'

It was Sergio this time. 'Mr Savage, you're honouring us. What makes you so sure we can deliver for that prestigious venue?'

'You're familiar with Sydney and the arts, Sergio, and an exhibition on such an iconic site is exactly what your group needs to bring your message home. You're an acclaimed sculptor, Sergio. I believe it's a good match. So, it's not unthinkable. I'll see what I can do.' At this point Brandon shook hands with their group and some of the other Valley Artists came over to discuss the possibilities. Amy was becoming more certain of the path their group was on and now they only had to convince the rest of the valley.

INTRUDER

She saw him through the crowd, a sleek figure lifted above the rest. His movement was sure and easy in the way he always held his place, privileged by power. He stood back from the stalls and observed with disdain. When one of the Manning children scudded by on their bike, throwing up dirt, he looked disconcerted having to step out of the path. It mustn't have been easy for Mark to figure his way through a group he had no control over, who were a bit mayhem in the face of his obvious finesse. It wasn't easy for Amy either to witness her ex-husband in her territory now. The danger signals were ringing. Why was he here? Whose mission was he representing? And most importantly why was he alone and without the woman he had left her for?

Dusty moved beside her and put his arm around her shoulder. He'd seen where her eyes were leading and how she stood transfixed. 'Are you alright, Amy? You look like you've seen a ghost.' Her heart was working into her rib cage so far that she felt faint. Who she had become, since arriving at The Retreat, hadn't been tested until now and the sudden confrontation of witnessing her ex-husband in all his righteousness had her unsettled and shaking.

'I just need to breathe a little slower. There's someone I need to talk to.' She had clung to Dusty's hand for reassurance, then a gradual easing came with an acknowledgement that she was ready. 'I won't be long.' Amy was sure Dusty watched as she made her way across the grounds and in between the stalls selling plants. She was sure he let her go because he knew she needed to face this moment alone. She took the woman who had grown up into the simple 'Me' the retreat had released. She took a heart that had healed in the wilderness to face a practised chameleon.

When Mark turned he didn't hesitate in his smooth connection. It was his usual trademark. 'Amy, I heard you were up here now.

It's good to see you. It's been a while.' There was no sign of the past in him. No remorse in his action to have discarded her so completely. Just the TAG Heuer on his wrist that he'd got for his last birthday with her, as a sign of the time between.

'What are you doing here, Mark? I can't remember you wanting to come up into the country in the fifteen years I knew you.' Her tone had lost the subservience he'd drawn out from her before. For a moment he caught the Amy he knew before they were married. Willful, yes she'd been willful once, always wanting what she couldn't have. That whining tone had come after he'd put her in her place. If only she'd fought more. It could have been interesting.

'Why so suspicious?' He looked almost conciliatory for a moment but then his expression changed and his demeanour carried a storm of resentment. 'You look like you've changed a lot, Amy. Bit too old for dancing like that though, don't you think? You don't want to let yourself go completely now.'

And then she realised he'd been watching her all along. She could feel gravity forcing her into submission in her usual response to him. The look of disdain that said, 'Really, Amy, you actually looked a bit of a fool.'

The way to let go is simply to fall from the edge and trust that you can float and not fall. And that's what happened when she realised the man she had once loved and probably still did, had never really seen her at all. His reason for marrying her was more unknown to her now than the woman in white who had come as a warning to halt her. She'd wasted a lot of herself in denial and she wasn't about to let it happen again.

'Goodbye, Mark. There's not much more we've got to say to each other, I think.' She meant it.

'Actually, Amy, I'll see you later. There's a meeting tonight and I believe you're chairing it. Might pop in.'

'The meeting is for the residents. Not outside interests.'

'Well, there's one resident who's not happy about what's happening here. He's invited me to come. But don't worry.

Nothing's going to change, yet. You'll still have some time in your paradise. For God's sake, Amy, wake up!'

So, he'd come to check out his client's opposition. The property down the road from Beth and Sergio's place had been sold only last year to an unknown buyer. They'd never been seen in the valley and the locals said the manager they had appointed kept to himself, not interested in doing anything with the property. Amy wouldn't have put it past Mark to have been in collusion with the owner right from the start. She should have suspected it earlier but there was no denying the man she was seeing now was efficient in his purpose. The law firm was on the side of the mining company and Mark held the law in his hands.

'I think you'd better bugger off, Mate.' It was Jack standing beside Amy now. His size equalled Mark's and was added to with the authority of years and a no nonsense approach. Jack was picking Mark up and escorting him to his car with just a flip of his head and the direction of his eyes to get out and leave her alone. Amy could only observe. Clothes didn't make the man and Jack had seen too much of rubbish that was buttoned inside it, to be outfoxed by Mark.

'Look, old man…'

'No, you look. The people here care about each other and we care about Amy so you had better let me know your business before the people here want to know your business too. They might not be as kind as I am.'

'Jack, this is my ex-husband, Mark Bentley.'

'Oh, of Harrison and Partners at Law. Yea, I know you alright. And I don't have to guess what you've come for.'

'Well, now it's Bentley and Harrison at Law, and what I'm here for is the meeting tonight. So, I'll see you both then.'

Amy watched as the BMW drove out of the gates. She watched as he spun the wheels on the cattle grid, the dirt splattering up onto the back window. He'd braked awkwardly and got out hurriedly to examine the car, dancing around like a boxer in the face of some unknown opponent. He seemed flighty. That wasn't like him at all.

'The plot thickens then. Looks like we're all in this together to fire the slingshot at the giant. Come on, Amy, Dusty will want to know all that has happened.' Jack was excited but all she could hear in her mind that made any sense was, 'Phone Barry Delany.' What she really needed though was more faith in her plan.

FIRST GATHERING

Beth and Sergio's home sat on a hill overlooking a wider section of the river. After the market, the locals had gathered to discuss the plan that Amy was proposing. She needed the rest of the valley residents to understand how together they could secure their future. Liam's job was to report on the meeting and he also had brought the sketchpad along to hold its memories. He thought of the first opening of the Australian parliament with all its ceremony and status and imagined this first gathering of valley residents would be quite the opposite in its casual friendliness and egalitarianism. Eileen said she could take photos to record the moment and Jack and Dusty sat beside Amy in the red armchairs assembled in the hosts' lounge room.

The house was large and open spaced with high ceilings and timber beams. A totem pole, into which Sergio had carved a tracery of leaves and vines from the property, held up the main structure. The locals gathered excitedly, the meeting disjointed at first as they greeted each other informally. The Manning and Davidson children sat on the stairs that led up to the first floor bedrooms, with the smallest of the Davidson's asleep in his brother's arms. The Bianchis distributed leftover pizza through the group who were standing and chatting aimlessly, until Amy called for the meeting to begin.

'Firstly, I want to acknowledge the traditional custodians of the land on which we gather and pay respect to the elders past, present and future. This valley is recognised by all of us here as our lifeblood. We understand that if we don't take care of it, then we are doing harm to ourselves as well. But we're living in a world that takes advantage of resources which may not be for our sake but for the sake of others who have big pockets. The individual has very little power over systems that favour the bigger investor. Our small farm holdings are ripe for the picking. I asked you here tonight to consider how we might act as one voice to keep what we have and yet add value as well to what we can do here in the future. I asked you here tonight to create a space for our valley and its residents to flourish, instead of succumbing to outside pressure and let mining have carte blanche.'

Amy was fervent and Liam saw Gino Bianchi nodding his agreement to his wife. 'It's the little people they come after. Since I come to this country I can breathe the air and feel free to bring up my family but now what will happen to us?' Gino looked around, hands in the air in question while his wife stood beside him quietly nodding.

'They buy you off. Or you can stay and sit beside the mine if that's what you'd prefer. I know that we'd be gone for sure and the neighbours would be lost from each other.' Mr McCaffrey, his arm around his wife, looked scared at the prospect. 'Our coffee business is doing well. We sell into the major cities now. I'm not sure I can start again in another valley. Our organic signature is vital to our success.' Ian McCaffrey was not only doing his sums. His children had made good friends at the local school. With a breakup of families, the school would need to close. Liam sketched the shape of the meeting as a continuum of concern. He drew dark lines around eyes that tried to focus to the centre where Amy and Jack sat but also captured those eyes lost to the ground where their fears lay.

'What's Jack got to say then?' George Fischer had come up from Boat Beach to attend. 'You've been here as long as I have, Jack. We've seen a lot of what the river has done for us over generations. You on the hills and me on the coast. What do you think we should do?' George had fished the estuaries for eons, his supply dependent on clean water. As much as the rest of the farmers, he had a stake in managing the ecosystem. His steely eyes had seen the tides and storms come and go and he had survived the worst of them. Jack knew that his were the eyes that had discovered David under that tree. He stared at George in a moment of recognition. They may not have seen each other often but the bond they held was unbreakable.

'All I've got to say, George, is to accept that we have a right as much as anyone else. We might not have been here first but we care about what we've got. It's not ours as you all know but we look after it for the future. If we speak with one voice we've got more of a chance.'

Eileen's camera had George Fischer in focus. The close up was of a sea worn face, a face she'd seen before many years ago. She'd been there on Boat Beach with David before he went away. George had been younger then when he locked the oars and rowed to sea over the swelling waves. David had spoken of how Jack and his mate George had fished together when the family went to the coast for holidays. How George would cook the flathead on an open fire and flirt with Mary with his sea tales until Jack would say, 'Enough' and the family would head back to the cabin they always rented. The cabin David had brought Eileen to.

She put down the camera and made her way toward him. Would he remember the shy girl David had introduced him to that night by the fire? The meeting hovered above her but some sense of David kept her pushing through the crowd to where George stood near the back wall. He watched her come. He'd seen the flash in his direction and understood that the woman Jack had spoken of, was the girl whom David had loved. Jack shared the beach with David but it was George who took him to sea. It was George who had saved his life.

'Excuse me, Mr Fischer.' Eileen was whispering. She didn't expect her young self could be kept in his memory from that night of storytelling as the embers lifted and she had seen her David's eyes light up with them.

'It's David's Eileen, I know.' He bent to kiss her and the touch of the past was left to warm her cheek.

'Mr Fischer, d'ye remember that night then?'

'It's the last time I saw David, Eileen. He was special to me too. He liked to come fishing with me.' He smiled as he looked back into the times David would sit and help him mend the net while

Jack and Mary strolled along the beach hand in hand. 'I miss him you know.'

'Did he say somethin' to ye? About m'self?' It was one more piece. A piece she might be able to place in the fracture of her heart that had been broken. A piece that David might have left behind to wash up on the beach for her to find.

'He told me he would marry you, Eileen. When he returned. He said he knew straight away, the minute he met you.'

'But sure how did he know? Did he say?'

'He said you were gentle, Eileen. That was all he needed to know.'

She held his hand then and the two of them stood with the swirling voices around them.

'Eileen, I had no son. I would wait for the holidays you see.' George stared towards Jack who sat with Dusty and Amy at the front. 'I think he went walking with Mary to give me time.'

'Time for what, George?' Eileen knew, she just needed him to say it.

'Time for David to be mine for a short while I guess. A time for a chance for love.'

'He needed me to go there with him, George. I think that tells ye what ye needed to know.'

MARCH OF THE PLANET

Liam drew the figure as a wolf. Flashing eyes in the dark of the corner. He was standing at the back of the room. Amy hadn't seen him as yet. Mark Bentley was taller than most and the group had unconsciously left him room, so he was exposed to anyone looking his way. His hands in his pockets kept him reserved to himself and his smirk suggested that he felt his place was more significant to those around. Dusty had seen him too and Liam could see him thread his way towards Mark with a determined stride.

Amy looked at the two men who were now locked together. The stakes included who had just rights to the valley. If it was Mark, she would be defeated on all counts. If it was Dusty, her plan had a chance of success. It was who could be the most convincing when it came to the residents and their needs. Liam sketched the two of them encircling each other, with heads down and butting horns. The two swimming in opposing agendas. It was Amy though who took the lead.

'I'd like to introduce Mark Bentley of the law firm representing the mining company. I believe Mr Bentley's been invited to this meeting by someone who is absent himself.'

'Couldn't face us, eh?'

'Shame on you!'

The locals were calling out but kept a check on any hostility. Mark walked to the front and locked eyes on Amy who sat relaxed in her position. It seemed to unnerve him and he looked away from her and toward the group. Liam wondered what hold Mark had over her in the past when Liam had come to see Amy's strength of conviction for the environment and her love for Dusty now.

'Frankly, I don't know what you lot are on about. The company has mining rights for exploration. There's actually nothing you can do about it and it will cost you money if you try. I can promise you that.'

'And what promise you make to the water, eh?' Mrs Bianchi had stepped forward for the first time. She was short and humble and often overlooked by others but this time Gino nodded in agreement. When it came to his wife, he knew whose voice resonated a power.

'All the environmental controls have been accounted for, I can assure you. Er, Mrs..?'

'Bianchi. Maria Bianchi's my name and I want you to know two things, Mr Bentley. I love my family and I love this valley. Who and what can you say you love, Mr Bentley?'

Mark looked towards Amy and back towards the softly spoken woman who'd stepped out from the crowd. 'That's not the point. I can appreciate your concern but we're talking thousands of jobs.'

'Perhaps.' Maria now was standing alone facing the giant before her.

'That's a bit vague, Mrs Bianchi. Have you any more to say than 'perhaps' or can we get on with pointing out the benefits?' It was like picking off goldfish.

'Perhaps you don't consider that we treat the land like we treat our children. We watch you see, Mr Bentley. We watch and we understand what it needs. Then we feed it so it can feed us. And when the rain comes we wait, Mr Bentley, until the floods wash through. It's like a cleansing, Mr Bentley. Do you know this mine is to be on a flood plain? What will be in the cleansing waters then, eh?'

'No disrespect, Mrs Bianchi, but it sounds a bit religious and not scientific at all. I think even God would have to agree with me on that one,' he sniggered.

The booing started with one fellow up the back and then filtered through the crowd until the entire room was booing. The Manning children were looking around excitedly to see democracy at work. Liam sketched madly to capture the uprising and although he felt sorry for a single figure being tossed about by a crowd, the mood was light-hearted rather than deadly and the image became a caricature of authority that had been pricked and deflated.

Amy then stood up and held both his hands in hers. Liam could see concern in her eyes and a meeting of a past that the rest of them had no understanding of. She led Mark out to the balcony while the others kept the uproar going, pouring drinks to salute their victory. Mrs Bianchi stood silently away from the others while the scene outside was of two figures in silhouette against the backdrop of the hills. If Liam hadn't known the story, they could be seen as lovers standing there in the moonlight. He wondered what Amy could be saying and what Mark could be hearing she meant. In a moment Liam saw them separate and then Mark walk away towards his vehicle. The sound of his car leaving brought up more cheers but Liam wondered what power they really had to quell the reach of Mark's firm in securing prospecting rights.

Amy returned and her eyes were red. Liam could see she'd been crying. It mustn't have been easy to stride between two worlds like she did but her intent was even more determined now. 'What we need is to make this valley an area of no access to mining. It's not just the buildings that make up an identity that matters. What our valley represents is a whole ecosystem of industry and integrated land use that together we can create. I propose we agree to form a company where the investors come to us for what we offer not for what they can exploit.'

'Bravo, Amy.' Eileen was the first to lead the applause. Liam knew the write-up for the paper needed the personal stories as much as the financial ones. He decided that he'd include his own story of the discovery of his new family and his place in the valley as well. Keeping a low profile was not beneficial to the task they were on and if the Valley Industry Corporation was to be born then it needed a strong presence in the city. He thought of the locals at the Opera House when the exhibition was set up and he could see the mix of city and country in the social pages. What they had to offer may be taken for granted but was not going to go unseen. Mrs Bianchi had been the catalyst for the change they needed, in all her quiet certainty.

The night air was moist as they retired to bed. Liam was in the guest house that opened to the night sky. From his loft bed he was able to watch the intensity of stars in a mesmerising flourish of light. A satellite beeped across the expanse, a tiny blimp that stopped and started in its ride. He wondered what they looked like from up there. The valley from space, along the east coast of a country removed from the rest of the world. How would their story make any difference to the march of the planet? He wasn't sure of the future but he was sure that each decision they took would have consequences. Jack had shown his grandson now enough of life, to know that those decisions needed to be approached gently and simply to mean anything worthwhile. Eileen was taking him canoeing in the morning and Liam longed for the moment alone with his mother when he could recover some of their lost time together as mother and son, when the consequences of past tragedies of war and forced adoption might find some peace at last.

PAPERBARK PEELING

Eileen watched as her son carried the boats to the water. He was unlike his father, having grown up in the city. Not as rugged in the way he moved, but how could he now with the different life he'd led and none of it his fault. He had her skin tone right enough, pale and slightly freckled but he also had David's long legs and blue eyes. He would fit in well back home that's for sure, she decided. She examined him like you'd examine a baby to see if everything was working. The baby who had been taken, now returned a man, was a gap in time she hoped to cross.

'Are you coming, Eileen?'

He was holding both canoes steady with the flow of water, gentle now at the side of the bank. Beth had told them to make their way to the Davidson property downstream where Dusty would pick them up. It would take a few hours and Eileen was hoping to see the kingfisher along the way as well. She would tell him the Irish story of it flying too close to the sun for its orange and its back to the sky for its blue. He'd learn it was the first bird out of the ark to find a new life. Then finally she would reveal how she would follow it as a child to help her find her way back home. She'd kept the story of her son alive in her heart but she questioned now where home for Liam really was.

Some of the cows from the property were drinking from the river, while others meandered their way on tracks through matt rush along the edge. Sergio and Beth had already milked in their small dairy before sunrise and Eileen thought, 'Tis not an easy life in the bush. You have to be strong like the red gum with its durable heartwood.' She witnessed that courage last night at the meeting, how they all gathered and came together to make a commitment to this wild river and their futures. She saw her son now as a part of the place that his father and grandparents, Jack and Mary, had led him to by some magic. 'Is it the rowan tree magic inside me now that has led me to this moment too?' she whispered to herself.

'Any instructions?' He seemed to want her to guide him although she suspected he knew more than he was saying.

'The trick is to keep paddlin'. It helps now to steady the boat, an' ye won't fall in come the rapids.'

'Will do, Eileen.'

He took his hand off his paddle to give her a salute. Then they hit turbulent water and Eileen watched as he struggled to correct himself. Dangerously he reached for a branch and she called out in fear for his safety. 'Let go of that, David. Sure ye can't hol' on to somethin' still when the waters are flowin' fast beneath ye. They can drag ye under.' She could tell there was no going back. They would have to ride this journey they were on with all its snags and open waters. She'd called him by the name that was in her all along. Now she wondered if he would accept the name she'd given him.

'Can you see the joey, Eileen?'

'A little baby is it? I haven't seen a koala in the wild before. At Taronga Zoo there were no babies when I visited.'

'Look at the pouch in the mother's abdomen. It will pop its head out if we wait for a moment.'

They pulled their canoes onto a bank and sat quietly to watch. The little joey crawled out of the pouch and scrambled onto its mother's back, clinging on tight as the mother crawled along the branch suspended high above them.

'It won't be long before it leaves for good and has to find its own habitat.'

His voice betrayed concern. It seemed to Eileen that time and the river was right for asking. 'Where might his thoughts be leadin' him now,' she wondered. 'Er, I need to ask ye somethin'. I've been afraid to speak of it before, but I'd be thankful if ye could tell me somethin' of the life you led.' She hesitated as his eyes lifted towards her. 'Were they good to ye? Yer parents, I mean now.' Her heart was knocking at the door of memory, apprehensive about a response that might exclude her forever.

'They were the best, Eileen. I was lucky. Brad and Jenny were kind and they always told me that I was their gift of life. I was their son.' His eyes had widened into a past Eileen had no idea of, nor place in and although she could hear his words of being safe and loved, they didn't comfort her. If she'd never been found by Dusty and if she'd never met her son, he would have been alright. She knew that it was herself who held the loss. She'd carried it in a scorched vessel across the years. The cross was her pain to bear. Because without it there was no David, no son of hers at all.

'It's OK, Eileen. They told me about the young woman they had driven to the hospital.' He'd been watching her too and wondering. 'They said the guilt had confounded them but they had no other way to be parents and the priest said it was alright. They believed they were giving me a better life.' He stalled as she waited. 'But sometimes they were whispering and didn't know I could hear. I heard them speak of the wailing down the corridor as they left the hospital and then they spoke of the sudden quiet.'

'They'd given me a needle to sleep.'

'I think they guessed that. There was no going back they said, so they did the best they could. I was a lot like them but then I was different, too.'

'How d'ye mean, different?'

'Well, it's something I've been wanting to ask you, Eileen.' He looked away then and held his head down as if to keep a distance from his question and his mother's reply. Eileen could see his body crumple into a self-doubt she didn't expect, nor had any way of preventing.

'Eileen, I feel I may not have been wanted. Is that right?'

She'd seen that shyness before, the uncertainty in how he saw his work. She realised then what they had not been able to give him. He was not like the heartwood of the red gum. He was like the paperbark which peeled away its soft skin in layers. Here was the layering of her son unpeeling before her and what could she say now to soothe him?

'I could see ye down a dark road, and sure here y'are now in the light. We have to accept, we two. All we have to do is accept.' Then Liam put his head on her shoulder and she held him in her arms like a mother and they were home together at last. 'Can I call ye David then? If ye wouldn't' mind now.'

'Can I call you Mum?'

The space around had closed. The river had supported their story as it lulled them along. Now the kayaks sat in the grass with native violet dotted blue in it. 'And what of Dad? Can you tell me about him?' She told him again about their time together before David went away. She told of how he might have known that a life was being left behind in her, to grow in his place if he never returned. He had made Dusty's dad know who his Irish lass was to make sure she was not forgotten. They were young and had found each other while a war waited. Time with his father was what her life had meant until now.

'Mum …' he paused to savour the word. 'I want you to stay on here you know. Jack has asked me to take over the property with Dusty as manager and I've decided to do my work from here, like Amy has been able to do. I need you Mum, to be my mum. I've already asked Dusty to help build you a cottage on the property if you'd be happy to stay on.'

Eileen then let go of the memory of working from dawn to pay her bills to the hospital. The lonely years of silence in her backroom flat. The searching through the city for a glimpse of his presence in every boy and man his age. She let go of the visits she'd made to Boat Beach to sit on the rocks and watch the young surfers catching the swells that rose up to crash eternally without David on them. She let go of Eileen who went from young girl to older woman, greying and frailer through the years. She wouldn't tell him of the prayers she'd spent, giving back their promise with their empty reply. She wouldn't tell him at all to worry him now, no not at all, now that he was hers.

There were old man banksias lining the river bank where Dusty was waiting to pick them up. The trees with their gnarled bark and serrated leaves looked like they had fought off many a bushfire. Red sap exuded down the trunk of one and the seed pods and hairy flowers stuck out like stoic chins defying any assault. Eileen called out to Dusty who stood in the shade of the tree where she could see above small birds flitting between the branches.

'What type of bird is it?' She was pointing to the flowers that stood like overgrown candles amongst the branches.

'It's the honey eater, Eileen. They're important for fertilization. They like to forage at the flower spikes.' He pulled the kayaks into the bank and was helping her out as Liam joined them.

'You know the honeyeater and the flower speak to each other. In colours.' Liam was grinning. 'They recognize each other's signals.'

Dusty smiled. 'Just like humans, huh? We're all connected in the end.'

SYDNEY

Harbour Bridge climbers inched skyward. Amy and Dusty's hotel room by the harbour had views to the Opera House and down Port Jackson to Sydney Heads. Amy lay in bed with Dusty asleep beside her. She watched the Manly ferry docking at Circular Quay, the early morning shift of workers emptying into the city in a syncopated beat. Dusty's frame sprawled across the bed as if to say the city wasn't big enough for him. He'd barely visited Sydney at all. Being here for the exhibition was a concession to their need to help save the valley, he'd said.

Brandon Savage had secured the prime spot for the exhibition as he had promised. The works of the Valley Artists were to line the perimeter of the foreshore and under the colonnades of the house that Utzon had designed back in the fifties. The elegant white sails of Sydney were said to have been built to enlighten a community. Amy knew that the Gadigal people of the Eora Nation had gathered on the land where 'the knowledge waters met'. She thought that somehow they'd been drawn to bring their story to this sacred place where the spirit and the stories of the first custodians still lived.

She thought of Jack in the room next door and how he must be feeling. His dream was being brought to the city to tell the story of the valley and its need for protection. It was weighing up whose voice had the strength to put the case for what progress meant. Jack had said that politicians had lost the plot when it came to the environment. That money was what drove decisions rather than good sense. It was a simple call but Jack was all about simplicity when it came to the truth. The profits from the mines were going offshore. 'They're laughing at us,' he said. Amy could see, though, that he was getting frailer with the effort and they'd decided to hire a water taxi to take him over for the opening. Dusty didn't want to admit it but Amy had seen Jack stumble a number of times and correct himself while holding on to a doorframe or chair, before he'd sit down and rest again for a while.

Sailing boats of all sizes tacked across the harbour. The maxi-yachts glided with an easy grace belying the effort of the sailors to precisely catch the wind and turn a hulking weight into a feather that could fly. She imagined one of the flitches back home being lifted from the bottom of the waterhole as the river swelled, to be carried along like one of those boats. She imagined it travelling through the valley and out to the sea beyond, to end up somewhere as driftwood on some beach for a child to gently pick up and carry home. To place that weathered timber on the windowsill and see the shape that is to be found in it. To dream that shape into its own story of survival, just like Jack had done.

'You look like you're in a daydream, Amy. Are you alright?' Dusty had woken and was already up and had his arm around her waist as she sat now at the window looking out over the harbour. 'You look like you've seen a ghost.' He pulled her to him and kissed her gently on the neck, the warmth of his body cocooning her concerns.

'It's Jack. I'm worried about Jack. He's getting frailer. Have you noticed?'

'It's hard not to. He's like an old war horse that won't lie down. I know it's not what we want to see but it's inevitable in the end.' He had that look of anguish that showed he understood far more than she did. 'That's why we need to finish the job we came here for. I want Jack to know we have made progress and intend to continue his legacy.'

The knock on the door came suddenly and strongly. 'Are you two up or what? You're missing the best part of the day!' Jack was his usual enthusiastic self, probably having been up for hours waiting for a civilized time to finally knock. Amy's thoughts of him weakening were lifted, as Dusty went to the door and let him in. He was holding the newspaper with the front page spread about the exhibition. The article sat alongside reports of the fireworks preparations for the next evening. The CBD would flood with people then, draining down alleyways and onto the foreshores, the steps of the Opera House wearing the party goers in a gown of expectation.

'Well, the time is right. All of Sydney and the rest of the country are either here or will be watching on TV.'

'Actually, Jack, the whole world tunes into the New Year's celebrations in Sydney. The exhibition opening the night before is just what we need to get our message out.' Dusty was grinning and Jack went quiet as he sat on the edge of the bed and contemplated.

'Mary would have loved to have been here. She would have been proud to see the work we've done ... the value of the environment being understood. I can feel they're here, Mary and David. Right here beside me now.' He patted the bed on either side of him and Amy pictured the three of them sitting together with their eyes towards the Opera House where Jack's reborn flitches were on display.

'We've booked a water taxi, old man, so you can arrive in style.' Dusty was being playful but Jack bucked in response.

'Who are you calling old, Son? I'll walk to the party if you don't mind.'

They laughed together but Amy could see Jack had meant it. There was no way he was being mollycoddled when he met the Mayor for the official opening. She looked to Dusty and there was an unsaid agreement that they'd take it carefully as they made their way past the cruise ships to Bennelong Point where the Opera House sat.

Jack opened the paper and there, in an interview, were Eileen and Liam telling their story. Liam had written the front page news about the reason for the exhibition and the corporate structure they'd managed to develop with the other property owners. It spoke about a model for ethical investment and urged people to visit the exhibition and then holiday in the valley as a break from the busy lives people led. The photo of the delta from the ridge at

The Retreat, showed a luscious food bowl. It was integrated with wildlife corridors and natural bush that Liam hoped Sydneysiders would grow to love. They just needed to take the time to recognise the intrinsic value of the place.

'Well, he's a smart fella alright. This story's a good one.' Jack was beaming as he held the paper and studied the words Liam had written. 'My grandson said he was taking me on a magical mystery tour this morning. Don't know what he's got in mind though.' He looked pleased with the idea of being led by Liam into a new experience instead of himself doing the leading. It was time to pass the reins. 'I think I'll just rest this afternoon … under a tree in a park maybe and watch life go by.'

Dusty went to the sofa where Jack was sitting and patted him on the shoulder gently. 'Well, I think you deserve that rest, Jack. Make it a good one. We want you fit for the big event tonight.'

MYSTERY TOUR

The mystery tour was a risk. Liam didn't know how Jack would take what it was he was about to show him. Liam had booked a taxi to take them up Elizabeth Street and drop them at the south end of Hyde Park. The ANZAC Memorial stood beside the Pool of Reflection. As Liam paid the driver, Jack stood staring at the poplars that lined the pool like silent guards.

'Have you been here before, Jack?'

'Just once when we were here for the Easter Show a long time ago. We brought David here to see some of our history. Mary's father had been at Gallipoli, you see. He was sixteen.'

'Wow, that's young. I didn't know. I'm sorry. Um, we don't have to go in if you don't want to. I'll understand.' Liam was angry at himself for spoiling Jack's time in Sydney. They'd come for a celebration and yet the yearning he had in him to share his dad's story with his grandfather was too real to let go.

'You going to write about this one then?'

'Not unless you give me permission. I came here as a kid on school excursion and the memory of the statue inside has been strong ever since. I had no idea I was connected at all to it.'

'How do you mean?'

'The Sacrifice Statue.'

'Don't talk to me about bloody sacrifice. More like sacrificial lambs. It wasn't our war to get into.' The past rose in him and Liam could see a pain there that he guessed had almost destroyed him. 'Mary put up with me though. She never gave up on me when I almost gave in. She just couldn't see it through for herself.' He hung his head for a moment and then turned to look at Liam who was holding back to give him room to speak. 'It was the anger. I had to tame the anger. If it wasn't for what I'd learnt up there in the bush, I don't know what would have happened.' He sighed then and let his breath come slowly as if his past was being carried away on its release. 'Alright then, David, let's see what it is you want to show me.'

They walked slowly then up the stone steps to the entrance and Liam held Jack by the elbow to make sure he was steady. 'Thanks, David. I don't like to admit it but I'm not as young as I used to be. Now, if I remember rightly, there should be your great grandfather's star on the ceiling.' The roof in the Hall of Silence was covered in a constellation of gold stars to commemorate the soldiers who had volunteered in the First World War. 'We picked that one at the top for Mary's father.' He was pointing and Liam followed his eye-line to one of the multitude of stars above the statue he had brought Jack here to see. Below, the figure of a naked youth lying on his shield with his mother and sister and wife holding him up, was almost too much for either of them to bear. The arms of the soldier were spread out across a sword that resembled a crucifix. Not a Peter Pan sword at all. One of the women was holding the young man's head in a gentle tension. Liam couldn't adjust to whether they supported him to be there or supported him because he was there. The reality of war was beyond his comprehension. What he had come to see was the baby in the mother's arms.

'That's me,' he thought. 'I'm the baby who was left behind. I'm the boy who never knew his father.' And then he realised it was everybody's story. Jack was seeing David and Mary. As Liam looked at him, Jack quietly wept. Tourists and visitors came and went like paper moths in their transparency, the pair silent, until it was Jack who finally moved.

'Well it's no bloody good, this remembering like this. My memories are back on the property where they stole my son. We begged him not to go but I had already raised him to do what was expected of him. I hadn't thought the decision could be taken out of our hands like it was.'

'You mean conscription, Jack?'

'Too right. Just think what it was like to sit by the TV at night and wait for your number to come up. The night David's number was picked out like a lottery, was the first night Mary quietly died inside. They didn't just take the son away. They took the entire family.'

'It's cruel, Jack.'

'It's cruel alright and useless. No-one won in the end. We're still fighting wars on other people's behalf. Now we have to fight to save our own way of life in the valley as well. It never ends.' He took a deep breath and looked out from the steps of the memorial. The Pool of Reflection mirrored the row of poplars ending with the Art Deco shrine. Two solitary figures of Jack and his grandson, David, stood at the top step like shadows captured in a net.

And then it was Jack who revived as he looked at Liam with a fear Liam recognised as survival. Somehow he was intent still on teaching him how to continue on, no matter what the circumstances. Liam was his grandson and Jack still had a job to do. 'Well come on then, Son, what else have you got in store for my mystery tour?'

Liam placed his hand on Jack's shoulder to take charge. 'Well, Jack, I thought you might like a boat trip.'

'Sounds like a plan. Let's go and catch a boat.' He was being conciliatory but Liam knew that the effect of the visit still lay heavily in his memory. Liam had stirred up the mud and now he hoped the wind and the sails would lift Jack's spirits.

The wooden yacht could take them out for a few hours to sail from Bradley's Head to Watson's Bay and back to sites around the harbour. It was a short sail and Liam thought a good idea for the both of them to enjoy the lift of the timbers under their feet and see the Opera House and their exhibition that was being set up for the evening's opening.

Captain Bradley sat Jack in the cockpit and signalled for Liam to man the ropes and lift the anchor. Jack spoke briefly to Bradley and then took over the steering. He'd done this before. The captain was calm, he and Jack sharing a private joke, the butt of which seemed to be on Liam. The sail was secured and the boat grabbed the wind and was off. Liam watched for instructions from the captain to tack across as they easily ducked ferries and other boats that lacked their expertise. Jack was at ease and Liam wondered what other surprises his grandfather had for him. It was Liam's idea to be on the water but as he had been finding out, life seemed to be leading him of its own accord anyway.

'Shift gears, David. The breeze is coming up!'

Jack stood, directing Liam to hoist the spinnaker as they jibed past Shark Island on the return run. On the port side, the Opera House was a hive of activities, with the marquee already up and the exhibition being assembled. Sergio's figure of a giant sea eagle sat on the prow of the foreshore. It cut out into the harbour, with its wings facing north towards the valley they had come here to protect.

'Look, Jack, they're setting up your work.'

'Watch out!' Liam hit the deck as the boom rushed past.

'Sorry, David. Didn't see the speed boat. Are you OK?' Captain Bradley had taken hold of the wheel and Jack was stricken with fear.

'No worries. Just need to keep my mind on the job. I think I was getting ahead of myself. I won't make that mistake again.'

Liam could see Jack visibly relax. For the rest of the sail, Jack sat without contributing, enjoying the lively colours and textures of a Sydney summer's day. As they disembarked, Liam waited for his explanation.

'David and I sailed in competition at the river entrance. We'd come close to qualifying for the Tokyo Olympics in the Flying Dutchman but when a storm came up we were disqualified.'

'What happened, Jack?'

'I had to make a decision to sail into the storm or keep safe. We hadn't seen a storm like it. The clouds had turned green and most of the boats pulled in. David wanted to continue but I pulled rank and said that we would wait it out on shore. He found it hard to forgive me and I found it hard to forgive myself but I couldn't take the chance on David being hurt. I didn't give a bugger about myself. All to no end though. The war took him anyway soon after.'

Liam could see his father as a man younger than himself and his grandfather as his age now. What decision would he have made to cross into territory he couldn't control?

'I used to say to David, if you don't take a risk you might as well be dead. I've blamed myself you see for putting that sort of recklessness into him.'

'You would have had no idea, Jack, of the forces operating outside your control.'

'I've learnt to be gentle with myself. It's the only way I've learnt to weather the storms then and since.'

That afternoon as Jack rested, he found a position under a tree in the park outside the hotel. His gaze seemed to stretch across the water into a place his grandson had no sense of. Liam had taken Jack into a whirlpool of memories and he only hoped that as the debris was drawn into the centre, Jack could stand to watch it swirl and wash away.

LOST BOY

Jack's gaze lifted across the harbour, over the bridge and into the forest he'd left behind. The mud had been stirred and now the ghosts came back to haunt him. His grandson had spoken of sacrifice, the offering of the self for something greater. The day that David went missing, Jack's self was all he had left to bargain with.

He recalled how his little son had said he'd seen the white butterfly dancing above his head like a fairy. Its wings must have moved in a rhythm to mesmerize his little boy who'd been told to wait a moment until his father came back. Jack remembered how David had said he could touch the fairy in the story that Mary had read to him at night but this time it was for real. Jack could see how David would have reached his finger out for more, eyes as wide as his mouth. He would never have been so close and so alone before with the tiny creature that David had said had jumped onto his nose to rest. Jack saw in his memory how he must have giggled as it flew, jumping from leaf to leaf along a path that led into its own direction and away from the path that he would look for him on.

The sky was turning crimson when he realised the inevitable, he recalled. David's little arms and feet must have been cold. It had been warm in the day and he'd played by the stream as Jack worked nearby. There was no need to put the shoes back on with only a lift onto his back to carry him home. But then the dark was coming in and the forest breath was turning blue. 'Daddy,' he must have cried again and again. 'I want my daddy.' But no answer had come as he stared into the trees above, the fingers of branches reaching upwards to a darkening sky.

Jack saw that David would have been hungry, when waiting back home was the soup in the pot that Mary had left when she'd gone to visit her sister on the coast. His little tummy would have grumbled as he cried for mummy too. But Jack believed, as if David could sense it would not help, that he had stopped his crying. The grass at his feet, being wet with the night, would have helped him with his thirst. His little mouth would have sucked the blades of grass which he pulled from the ground. And then when he ate the grass, green stains around his mouth could not have been washed away that night.

Jack began to imagine the danger scuffling past behind the trees nearby. The breaking sound of twigs as padded feet stalked silently. Instinctively, David must have known to calm himself before the creature could sense his fear and come for him. Above, the owl might have swooped past and risen into the branch above to look down to the place he could rest. The ghost gum would have glowed white in the moonlight. David had said he saw the lady in white with the umbrella branch which rose above him. He had said that he lay in the leaves at her feet and kept himself still and tried not to cry out.

Jack recalled that hundreds of people had come from the valley. He'd rung for help to the police and George Fischer had heard the call and was sure that Mary was not told. He'd said the people drove quietly past the house she was visiting in with her sister. But Jack suspected that a mother always knows when a son is hurt. Jack could see her still at her window looking out, her face white and desperate against the glass.

Then Jack entered further into time and saw David and his mate, Glen, scouring the bamboo with assault rifles in their hands. David, who'd learnt to be calm as a boy when a wombat came that night and lay by his side to keep him warm. David, who kept his breathing steady as he counted each step in the dark. His mate Glen had said that David was behind him, each searching for the guerrillas coming their way from all directions out of the shadows. Jack had been told that the moment was quick and loud and dreadful when David was poised to throw Glen to the ground and sacrifice himself instead. He was ready to stand and fight and take the bullet in the chest that he had no way to prevent in the end.

Jack could see his boy fall and turn his face to the sky. He pictured how Glen had stood by David until they were told to run. Glen had said there was no breath left, just the face of the boy in the man. Jack watched as the news returned home and Mary was told. He remembered how she shrivelled like a dying plant. They'd taken the truth and laid it in his bedroom beside the soft wombat toy he'd had since three. The toy that lay on top of his bed even now, with silent eyes staring into the cold air.

Then Jack saw the night he set the saw-mill on fire. Douse the timber, light a match and watch it burn. It ignited in the sawdust first, like a genie exploding out. He dropped the kerosene bottle as the length of the fire drew an arc from the ground to his fingers. Mary had been dead since morning. Faded away, like a little bird he'd tried to feed with a spoon. But her eyes were already sunk into the memory she couldn't shake. The memory of her boy walking away without return, the silence between them the widening crack that divided them. Not her fault at all, not his either. Just a simple loss which couldn't be replaced with time.

He'd lain by her side for days as she faded. A pup on the floor by her bedside. Devoted. Now not even his strength could pull back the covers and breathe the life back in. Only the silent waiting until the last. Taking each breath with hers until his was the only one left. The fire already in his mind to burn. To raze the ground of his own despair and empty the life he'd built for her, to ash.

Flames had rolled across timber roof beams until the corrugation fell in, the saw already hot with charring as it hit. Mary lay dead in the house beside the mill as Jack stood on the veranda and watched his life burn. The machine gun sound of helicopter, that metal dragonfly overhead, was landing too late. David was already gone, like Mary, and only Jack was left behind.

But wildfires happen too quickly and Jack recalled it was not his intention to destroy beyond his realm. Only the quickening wind could stir beyond the site and into the bush beyond. Here the wildlife lay quietly as the embers burned nearby. He remembered how the kelpie had pulled on him to come back, to grab the hose before the southerly sprung up.

And then again, the neighbours from the valley who rushed to help, scrambling up the rutted track to the house with the bushfire truck loaded with volunteers. They had put the fire out with Jack and Mary inside, with the kelpie, Joe, by their side. He could see through the window, the Manning boys beside their father, a team at the pump and the hose. Gino Bianchi with the axe, cutting through the timbers, separating the burning ones from the rest.

They took him back down the valley with Mary in the truck in the back. There were no words, just a readiness to be there and fight when needed. Beth and Sergio had fed Jack and his dog and they made him stay for a few days while the funeral was arranged. He understood it was all any of them could do, as they watched him go back with no idea if he would ever return.

Now Jack watched from the edge of the harbour. The self he'd offered up to save his family was still here when both Mary and David were gone. He saw the maxi yachts parading their tacking in wide turns as the smaller yachts pirouetted outside. The large and the small of it now was life and death to Jack. It came and went with the seasons, the big stories built from the smaller everyday. A kayaker threaded through the wash. He surged forward on the smaller wave and rode over the top of the bigger wash from the maxi, the skill of the paddler keeping the tiny craft afloat.

'Steady now,' he thought. 'Steady and keep paddling when the wave rises up. Turn into it, Son. Face it head on and don't go sideways now. Now stroke and put your back into it, David. Grit your teeth in the face of it, Son, then let go into the flow. Feel the rhythm of it now. That's it … the rhythm carries you. It carries me now to you.

WHAT TO DESTROY

Amy and Dusty walked with Eileen, David and Jack around the harbour to Bennelong Point and the Opera House. They walked through swelling crowds that swam together and apart like schools of fish. It seemed the whole world was represented at Circular Quay for New Year celebrations which started days before. Across the water, the bays were already playing host to parties. Some people were diving into the harbour and crawling back up rocks to summersault in again to cheers from strangers. Boats of all sizes paraded past in a dance that crossed and weaved a celebration. There was no hurry as people settled into the bars and restaurants with views across the waters. Various laughter came from cracks in conversations, down laneways and on tops of balconies. Lovers were already closing into each other. It was a time for love in Sydney, if only for a few nights for some.

Amy's life had changed since the Christmas two years ago when she had crossed on the ferry to her marriage ending. The year that followed nearly ended her and then the invitation to the retreat last Easter had resurrected a self-respect. Now she walked beside a man she loved and a family who had been reunited in a miracle. When she had sat at the Opera Bar with the secretary circling, she had no idea then that she could walk on the upper concourse to a new opening and a life with meaning. They took it easy walking past cruise ships, like docked cities on water. Tourists on the upper decks partied in their private lives on board while other more adventurous ones were already melding with the crowds below.

Amy could see that Jack was tired and several times they stopped to watch a street performer, to give Jack time to rest. The indigenous group playing the didgeridoo amongst the converging mobs was haunting and surreal. Amy couldn't fathom their presence, dressed in traditional costume, with the sales pitch to buy their CD. In many ways it was what they were planning to do at the opening. Ply their trade. Persuade people that what they had to offer was worthwhile. To take the bargain that the environment offered. A better life. Without protection of the environment, Amy knew, the life people led would be diminished, perhaps even inconsolably.

'Hey, Mista. Chao ong.'

A little girl with dark hair ran up to Jack with an ice-cream in her hand. She was offering him the cone to take while her parents looked on bewildered. They watched as Jack bent towards her and smiled, thanking her for her gift. Then he pulled out a small object from his pocket to exchange. It was a miniature stylised tree he had carved from a piece of flitch. He looked to the parents to ask permission. Their cameras and back packs identified them as tourists as they smilingly nodded the little girl could accept.

'Kam ung.' The child had become shy now as she backed into the fold of her parents, clasping the tree to herself.

Liam recognised the family as Vietnamese and spoke to Jack who looked shaken for the moment. The ice-cream dripped down his arm and Eileen handed him a tissue to mop it up. The Vietnamese family had moved on and Jack started to eat the left overs of the gift he had been given.

'Are you OK, Jack? Maybe you better sit down for a few moments.' Dusty tried to lead Jack to a seat that had a space left in all the crowds that were gathering.

'Thank you, Dusty, but I'm fine. We'll get to the opening. The sun's going down and we don't want to miss anything.'

They walked then along the harbour edge, in silence, as the clouds changed from reds to golds on the western horizon towards Parramatta. The bridge climb was quiet with the fireworks in preparation. No-one was sure how Jack would react. The child had picked him out from the crowd to give a gift. At one point they walked in single file to push their way through and not lose each other. Liam had his hand on Jack's shoulder just in case and Dusty led the way. In the curve of the harbour edge they were alone for a moment, beyond the ferry wharf where lines of people were gathered to cross to the North Shore or Darling Harbour or any of the other pockets of summer celebrations. It was as if Jack had been contemplating what to reply as they made their way towards the Opera House.

'They shattered the environment, you know. The bombing and the herbicides. We knew what to destroy to kill the people.'

'You mean Vietnam, Jack?' Liam was standing beside his grandfather with Dusty and Amy nearby.

'There are no winners, Jack. We're all losers in a war, that's for sure now.' Eileen had put her arm through Jack's and the family stood stoically together as the memories of David and Mary and all they had lost surfaced.

'It might not be a celebration we are going to but at least it can be a victory. The opening tonight at least is showing a different way to see things. And that's something.' Jack was being pensive and seeking reassurance that his dream could last.

'Just the simple steps, Jack. We're in this together and we intend to keep going. So, come on old man.' Dusty was grinning at Jack who looked at him with affection.

'Who you calling old again, Son? Haven't I taught you better than that?'

'Come on then, Jack. Let's see what the crowd thinks of your ideas.'

The Opera House stood before them in a flush of elegance, of white sails mirroring the colours of the sunset. At one point a peak of gold tipped the topmost sail and then disappeared into a greying night sky. The steps leading up to the main entrance were covered in people arranged like a ceremonial gathering.

'Bennelong Point has had people gathering here for tens of thousands of years and if you look over the edge into the harbour you can see the rocks that have been here for even longer.' Jack was pointing trying to give more of his ideas as if there was some urgency in what he had to say. 'I think this will be my last time in

Sydney. I've got too much to do back home. I'll have to prioritise.'

Dusty showed concern. 'You don't know that, Jack. Amy has more work to do on the proposal and will need to come here a fair bit. I thought we could come together.'

'Not for me, Son. That will do me. You lot enjoy it though. It's a beautiful city in this light. Isn't it, David?'

'Yes, Grandad. It sure is.'

'Will you paint it for me?'

'What would you like to see in the painting, Jack?'

He stood there then and thought about the times that they had come to Sydney for the Easter Show.

'I'd like the Manly Ferry with Mary, myself and David sitting on the upper deck looking out to sea.'

'I think I can manage that, Jack. Just for you.'

STONE IN HIS HAND

The argument below on the lower concourse where the Opera Bar was spilling with people, played out like a dumb-show. The suits and stilettos were intermingling, with the age divide apparent as per usual. Amy watched as if the years had wound back and it was herself below in the mix of it all. She signalled to the others to go on. She would meet them soon near the Drama Theatre where the exhibition was set up. Dusty could see where her eyes were focused and understood again that this was her story alone to examine.

The man had his back to the young woman who was trying to persuade him to turn around and face her. Some of the other men at his table were trying to usher her away but she broke away from them and stumbled towards the group. One of her stilettos seemed broken but she pushed forward anyway, through the crowd who parted to give her room. Amy could see the long black hair dishevelled and the tight cocktail dress looking brash in its attempts to please, the breasts pulsating further out than the two years before. She watched above the scene, where the music continued to play and people still danced and mingled. Waiters served tables and left the group where the fracas was happening, to themselves. They'd seen it all before. The days leading up to New Year's Eve were often accentuated in a champagne cork pressure. It was the reality of a place where the social and the domestic interlaced, which ended badly if life itself had become a lie.

Then there was a shove and the girl fell back onto a seat where she sat wildly looking around for someone to help her. Amy was thankful she hadn't come to physical violence with Mark like this, but the emotional trauma was always there. A bouncer arrived and Amy watched as Mark was led out of the bar and deposited on the concourse above, near her. She stayed still as he rumpled past, embarrassed, she guessed, by his slip-up to show a darker side he usually kept to himself. Sarah must have really challenged him to let it come to this. Maybe it was just that he was getting older and the old boss and new recruit were becoming too distant to matter.

She thought to call out. But she knew that his anger must be fuelled by now, with his usual drinking non-stop after work. She guessed he was on his fifth when he probably propositioned the new girl across the table. Amy guessed he had forgotten Sarah was near enough to hear. She would have seen the same game she had acquiesced to the years before, to make her way in the corporate world. He looked tired and beaten as he pushed through the crowds towards where the exhibition was about to open. Then, as if he had found himself going in the wrong direction, he turned distractedly to come back her way again. Their eyes met in a moment of confusion for them both. Amy kept still as if she were confronting a wild animal in the bush. Mark was calculating whether it was worth his time to stop and say hello or just ignore the fact he had seen his ex-wife at all. It was what he would have done if he had his senses about him but after the scuffle down below he was without his personal shield of nonchalance.

'So, I guess you saw what happened. Moral justice you think?' His first words were on the attack, his usual defence.

'I felt sorry for you, if that's what you mean.'

Mark eyed her sideways as if her old sentimentality, which he'd found cloying, was on display. Amy continued to hold her distance. There was no coming back and no desire to be one of those women at the bar with a husband who was having an affair with the woman beside her. What she did desire was an understanding of how she got onto that conveyor belt in the first place.

'Maybe it's time to say sorry yourself, Mark.'

'Sorry for what? To you, you mean?'

'Well, perhaps to anyone your actions have harmed.' She was direct, perhaps for the first time. She wasn't expecting him to act but she was expecting to speak for herself.

'You really are a fool, Amy. As if anyone would want you. Good luck with that.'

He turned away from her then, trying to hold his head up as he pushed away, but a bigger man in a leather jacket shoved him back as he bumped into him. It wasn't going to be a happy night for Mark. Amy could see the crumpled suit was tight fitting on his expanding waistline. Middle age had caught up it seemed. Amy wondered what was happening in the firm to catch him off guard so much.

She realised there was this chance to call out. To search for the man she once knew. 'Mark, about the mine?'

He turned then to face her again and this time his look softened as if he'd lost his way and needed anything to hold onto. 'It's off the table for the moment. But we'll be back. It's just a matter of time.'

'Thank you, Mark.'

'Why are you thanking me, Amy? I'm the last person you need to thank.' For the moment he was the young David in Florence who she imagined him to be, with the stone in his hand ready to take on the giant. Which way he was to throw it in his sling was up to him.

'Goodbye, Mark. If you need some time off, there's a bed for you at The Retreat. You only need to call.'

'Yea, well we'll see about that.' He emptied into the crowd like the apparition that had dissolved in the forest. Amy could only guess where his night might lead and which direction he'd wake to in the morning.

YEARNING

The opening to the exhibition began with Jack's flitches turned into an installation of trees that spread through the site. At the base of each tree Jack had planted a city high-rise, diminished now in size in comparison. Like a theatre set that suggested an open space to play out the drama, his high-rise were unfinished, with walls that were half formed that were open to the sky. They were not derelict but suggestive about what growth they were to take.

The tree at the entrance had children playing in it, the boy dangling from his knees on a lower branch, the girl climbing to the top branch to see out. 'That's you, David and Amy. I hope you both like it.' Jack was grinning, pleased with the secret he'd kept to surprise them, being revealed now against the backdrop of the harbour lights. Jack remembered what his grandson had told him about playing in the tree in his city street and Dusty had listened to Amy tell of the dreams she had when she was a child and relayed them to Jack. The times when she climbed to the top of the tree in her street to be closer to the sky, was a yearning she had to come home, she'd said. She found it with Dusty and Jack and the community in the valley. They were all waiting inside. Jack could see the Manning family and their children, the McCaffreys, the Bianchis, the Davidsons and George Fischer sitting on an upturned fishing boat with sand sculptures nearby.

'You did this, George?' Jack was curious as to how his old mate had managed to make such life like fish.

'The truth is, I had a bit of help from a professional but the idea is that kids can play here and make their own. I'm happy if these fish are knocked down in the morning. They look the part tonight though.' He paused then and shifted uneasily, 'Not like me in this get-up.' George had already loosened the tie he was wearing and started to untie it completely to put it in his coat pocket. 'Haven't been in one of these hob-nob outfits since my wedding and that was so long ago I've forgotten.'

'You've done yourself proud, George.' Dusty patted him on the shoulder as Beth and Sergio came over to lead both older men to the podium where chairs were set up for the special guests.

Invited dignitaries were moving through the exhibition. Dusty hoped that Brandon Savage had done his homework and included people who understood the value of the environment as well as those who needed to. He hoped the conversations they had, would help when decisions were being made about what was important for the environment and for their own health.

When the family joined the mayor who was standing with Brandon Savage, Melanie and her friend Sam were playing a song under the colonnades. Melanie had composed a song with Eileen in mind and the lyrical meandering and circularity had everyone tapping their feet to the rhythm.

'That's the sound of my childhood, David.'

'It's a sound I could get used to, Mum. We've got a lot of catching up to do. Maybe we'll visit Ireland next year.'

'Next year starts tomorrow, David.'

'Well, I'll make sure to buy the tickets tomorrow. Dublin here we come!'

They were both laughing and Liam was holding his mother by the hand as he led her to a seat beside Jack and George. The mayor had been introduced by Brandon but now she looked towards Liam for confirmation that they both had similar reasons for being here. She had fought the developers on numerous occasions but had lost the fight with the Barretts and others with powerful interests. The truth was, though, that the city was becoming tired of being browbeaten. People were demanding more say in how planning decisions were going to affect them and the media was beginning to voice both sides of the story more fairly.

'Mayor Lindsay, this is Jack Turner. He's had a lot to do with trying to convince people that the valley should be hands off to mining. I'm proud to say he's also my grandfather.' Liam was pleased to be able to introduce the mayor, a woman he had had many previous encounters with, to the new family he had embraced.

'I'm pleased to meet you, Jack. Your grandson has kept me honest on a number of occasions.' She grinned at Liam in memory of the battles they'd had over the rezoning laws the Barretts had taken advantage of and her inability at that stage to defeat it. She'd won the next round though and no new development was to have exclusive right over the public access to the harbour. Jack was ready for a fight of his own and responded quickly to the introduction.

'Well, he's David to us, Mayor Lindsay. Regrettably, we weren't there to instil his values but it gives us hope in the way he was brought up, that there are many people out there who understand the message we are speaking about. Mining a valley that provides drinking water and wild-life habitat is against all common sense. We need laws to protect the people, the land and the animals who depend on it for survival.' Jack was outspoken but controlled his delivery.

'As you can see, Jack is determined. We won't be giving up this fight. There's too much at stake.' Liam was standing beside Jack now with the conviction that whatever was needed to protect the valley he now called home, he was ready too.

'I can hear what you're all saying. It's the same for Sydney. We're all for sustainability. It's taken us a lot of effort but we've been cleaning up the harbour and finding new ways to green the city. We know it's vital for the health of the people and important for the tourists as well. So we've all got a stake in this, Jack. It's not just the valley residents. That's why I was so pleased to be able to open this exhibition. The whole world's on edge about the environment and its need for protection.'

Eileen recognised the mayor's passion. She squeezed Liam's hand for an introduction. 'And this is my mother, Eileen. We're getting to know each other as well. Mum was one of those women caught up in forced adoptions in the 60's.'

'I'm very pleased to meet you, Eileen. I'm sorry to hear that both you and Liam were part of that tragedy. I have great affection for your son. He's done a lot of good work here in Sydney over the years.' The mayor had turned towards Liam and smiled. Their eyes locked in recognition and for the first time he let them linger there, not as a reporter but as a friend. Eileen saw the ease in which they kept company and decided to plant a seed of her own.

'Well, maybe one day ye could visit. Anne is it? I think David would love to show you the valley. Wouldn't ye now, David?'

'I think I could manage that, if Anne would agree.' Standing amongst family and friends, with his paintings of light on water already being sold to enthusiastic buyers, Liam allowed himself to accept the interest from the mayor, a woman who had been trying to get him to notice her for a very long time.

'Well, what about next Sunday then? I could drive up and meet you at the markets I've heard so much about.'

'No, not at all now. Sure, David would be pleased to come and pick ye up, Anne.' Eileen was smiling at her son, happy that she could give him some instruction on how to treat a woman, a mother's instruction that she'd never had the chance to give before.

'Of course, Anne. It would be my pleasure.' It was then that the roles of journalist and mayor dissolved and a quiet man took a chance on love.

The swelling harbour full of boats and parties held court to the little tribe of locals from the valley who sipped champagne and toasted to the effort they had all made to get there. Sergio's other work consisted of birds' nests he'd sculpted. The central nest was a sculpture of Centre Point Tower that he had shaped into an eagle's nest for the bird that braced the harbour. Where the wild and the civilized blended was hard to distinguish. The work of the valley children was also on show. Beth had organised the children to tell their stories of playing in the river and video installations of these stories could be seen on several outdoor screens.

Jack mingled through the gathering like the captain of the ship. The Opera House sails rode majestically overhead while Jack charmed the doyens of Double Bay and harbour-side mansions who had bought his work before. Many were convinced to join in a retreat when they could find the time. 'It's simply marvelous, Jack. The whole thing. It's simply marvellous.' One woman, who'd drunk too much, was gabbling about the animals and the fish and the butterflies and, 'What would we do without all the water?' before someone quietly led her inside the colonnades and into the ladies restroom to cool off.

At nine, fireworks erupted in a dress rehearsal to the following evening when you wouldn't be able to move where the private party gathered now. The painting of the sky with rockets, melted light over the bridge and the Opera House and settled into the harbour in splattering rainbows.

'It's bloody marvelous, Jack. But I've seen it all before.'

'Yes, George. What's say you and me catch that water taxi home now and leave the party to the kids?'

Eileen, standing beside them agreed. 'Well I'd like to join yis. I've had a wee bit too much fun as it is.'

As the fireworks ended, Jack, George and Eileen were seen off in grand style by strangers who hollered, 'Save the forests! Bring on more champagne!' Dusty made sure they had their hotel swipe-key and reassured them that the evening was really a success. 'If it wasn't for you, Jack, we wouldn't have been drawn to this place to tell our story.'

'I don't think it's got anything to do with me, Son. We're being pulled along by something far greater than ourselves you know.'

'What's that, Jack?' Amy was quietly listening.

'You tell'em, George.'

'By life, Amy. By life, my dear.'

GENTLE

The little taxi made its way across the bay to the hotel on the water, its small size anonymous as it passed by luxury yachts and ocean liners decked with party lights and pulsating rhythms. The three passengers sat quietly together as Sydney swirled around them. The tide was beginning to suck and pull out to sea. The driver throttled the engine to gain more power until finally cutting the engine as it pulled up to the hotel dock, the momentum of the boat coming to rest as it countered the current until the ropes were moored.

'That's a smooth entry, Mate.' George was impressed with the careful way the driver balanced the wash from the flotilla of boats parading past.

'Might be able to get a job yourself, George. You've had enough experience at sea. What do you say, could you live in the city do you think?' Jack was playful in his teasing. They both knew where their home lay, a few hours north in the quiet reaches of their river valley.

'No, Mate, she'll be right where I am I think. I couldn't give up my night sky for this. These fireworks are beaut alright but they've got nothing on the spread of the Milky Way, which you can't see properly from here.'

'What do you think then, Eileen? Do you miss Sydney now you live up with us?' Now Jack was being careful. He wanted Eileen to understand that she had choice in how and where she lived.

'It's a blessin', Jack, but I'll also be comin' and goin' to the city with David, I think.' She looked conspiratorial as if the secret she had just discovered was too much to keep to herself. 'David's takin' me home to Ireland, Jack. I'd like to take you with us, if ye'd say yes.' She could see his eyes widen to take in a world he had little experience of. 'Sure Dusty and Amy could look after the place for a wee while. What d'ye say now, Jack?'

Jack smiled at the thought of all the world he hadn't seen but imagined was out there. His world had been confined to the little valley on the coast. He knew its river run through the seasons. The way the barks fell and the seeds grew. He knew the owl was waiting on his veranda post for his return. He'd wanted more at one stage when he cut through the landscape to make his mark but now he was content with the vines creeping back and his place down amongst the growth. 'We'll see, Eileen. I'll have to consult my diary first.'

Later in his room alone, Jack thought of the diary that had occupied his thoughts. He'd always looked ahead steering the ship towards an inevitability he had no control of. What he had discovered though was how he could approach that fate, with a steady gaze towards the horizon. The silk curtain covering the window which overlooked the bridge and the harbour lifted invitingly and Jack recalled Eileen saying, 'There's somethin' special for us all to see out there tomorrow night.' She'd said the mayor and David had it as a secret.

The breeze had come up and with the balcony door slightly ajar, the curtain opened now in a quiet presence. What had Eileen meant when she and George had smiled so knowingly? She'd left with an intention, 'I'll just open this door a wee bit fer ye now. Fer sure, some fresh air will d'yer good.' It was a simple effort for him to get up and close it now.

Outside the harbour had quietened, all the boats asleep in their moorings except for a singular water taxi crossing silently towards North Sydney. He followed its trajectory across the hull of the bridge, which rose from the water like a ghost ship lit up from below. He knew that later the bridge would hold waterfalls of light as the New Year's celebration would come to an end. His flitches then would be returned to the valley and life he hoped would return to normal. But now there was the story of the city to consider. The people who came together in connecting arteries of density. How did they find their space amongst the rush of it all? And yet Jack knew that they must. That in every constriction, a new space was created diminishing in size to infinity.

He thought of the young girl who'd come to him with an ice-cream in her hand. The tree he'd exchanged standing near where she slept perhaps. The little gifts of touch we give each other are all we have left to treasure in the end, he thought as he lent further into the wind that was rising now. The steel arch of the bridge suspended above him and cast away, drawing his eye along its highway north. An outline of letters, were attached to its side like barnacles. And then as if the bridge was delivering its message for his eyes alone, before it lit up that night in a climax of fireworks for all the world to see, Jack realised the meaning that the letters connected.

Eileen had said it was a secret, yet Jack knew the secret was within us all. David had said the mayor was planning a surprise and Jack thought how a surprise can come slowly like a sunrise when you're ready for it. And then the sunrise can be savoured as Jack savoured what was before him in the darkness. The chair on the balcony was wet with dew but he sat anyway to look. Eileen was right. In the crush of a New Year's Eve party, the word 'Gentle' would not come to him then in comfort, as it did now in its silence.

EPILOGUE

The morning Jack died, the clouds had built up while the family was sleeping. Clouds boiled and a purple haze settled in to shift and change colour. The river mirrored the changes and a series of rainbows fell in sheets towards the ground. Lightning bolts arched and white cockatoos flew like confetti across the greying build up. Finally, the rain started and fell like a tropical storm, heavy and drenching. A whisper brushed past as if in a dream and it was gentle and quiet against the storm. It emptied itself into the distance and rolled away like the edge of thunder.

Then the barks changed colours from greens to blues as rain fell like tears, settling into rivulets that dug through the soil, etching their way to the river. An old flitch from a log, lay like dead man's whiskers below the surface. It lifted then from the bottom of the waterhole as the river swelled and was carried along like a boat, spiralling with eddies as it coursed along the bank near the retreat. And then as if to travel straight, it turned its elbow east and was carried away through the valley and out to the sea beyond.

The house that had been shut up lay quietly, a museum of past life suspended until now. The house that Jack had built for Mary and David stood silently in time. The day David had left there had been a slow dying away. The story of a family lost to a war that had come up into their quiet valley to hunt for them. Today they'd found the key to the wooden door by Jack's bed and entered solemnly. The dankness had grown along with the weeds. Dusty, who entered last, secured the door to the latch as the air rushed through like a gasping breath.

The long corridor welcomed the line of light that entered in, creating archways of light that opened into rooms on either side. To the left, Mary and Jack's bed lay with a picture of the Sacred Heart, dressed in thorns, above it. Liam wondered who his grandparents must have been when young, to place a sorrowful heart above a wedding bed like that. Was it a faith that continued on in David, a faith that carried him so far away from home? Liam drew the yellow curtains and sunlight spilled across the bed and up the walls. He watched how the light caught the mirror on the dresser and he imagined the faces of the past still there. Mary putting on her lipstick for Jack's return. His father, David, playing on the bed beside.

Dusty had opened the bedside drawer and his father's handwriting became distinguishable on the letters inside. He gathered the bundle to take them to read as he knew Jack would have wanted. Amy stood back to witness how each letter was examined for dates that meant something. She watched as Dusty fingered each one like a lover, gently and quietly. Then she let him go as he opened the door to the veranda and stepped outside.

Eileen entered first into David's room. The soft toy lay still on the pillow facing the door. The room was already fresh with the window ajar at the top, quietly opened to the sky. Eileen thought about David leaving it open to dream. She imagined him packing his bag to walk away to war, his parents by the front door waiting. He'd left his civilian clothes in the closet, hanging in the shape of the man. Eileen lifted the blue jacket he'd left behind and drew it to her now, her cheeks wet against the sleeve.

Outside the kookaburra, the great brown kingfisher, was tending its nest in the womb of the gumtree, the fledglings inside scrambling with each other to fly. Amy had come to the retreat to hold to sanity when the world around was spinning. She saw how Dusty sat watching the tree as a small bundle of hope perched itself on the eucalypt branch, ready to step off. She knew she was ready to take that leap too. She'd come to the valley to find her way. And now this simple thing. This point of gentle balance.

ABOUT THE AUTHOR

Cate grew up on the east coast of New South Wales where this novel is set. She enjoys the natural beauty of the river valleys and coastline of this beautiful area and hopes her voice contributes to the careful management of the environment. Cate studied Creative Writing at Macquarie University in Sydney. *Gentle* is her first novel.

www.ingramcontent.com/pod-product-compliance
Lightning Source LLC
LaVergne TN
LVHW051559070426
835507LV00021B/2662